# Human Frailty

# 33 1/3 Global

**33 1/3 Global**, a series related to but independent from **33 1/3**, takes the format of the original series of short, music-based books and brings the focus to music throughout the world. With initial volumes focusing on Japanese and Brazilian music, the series will also include volumes on the popular music of Australia/Oceania, Europe, Africa, the Middle East and more.

## 33 1/3 Japan

Series Editor: Noriko Manabe

Spanning a range of artists and genres from the 1970s rock of Happy End to technopop band Yellow Magic Orchestra, the Shibuya-kei of Cornelius, classic anime series *Cowboy Bebop,* J-Pop/EDM hybrid Perfume and vocaloid star Hatsune Miku, **33 1/3 Japan** is a series devoted to in-depth examination of Japanese popular music of the twentieth and twenty-first centuries.

Published Titles:
Supercell's *Supercell* by Keisuke Yamada
*AKB48* by Patrick W. Galbraith and Jason G. Karlin
Yoko Kanno's *Cowboy Bebop Soundtrack* by Rose Bridges
Perfume's *Game* by Patrick St. Michel
Cornelius's *Fantasma* by Martin Roberts
Joe Hisaishi's *My Neighbor Totoro: Soundtrack* by Kunio Hara
Shonen Knife's *Happy Hour* by Brooke McCorkle
Nenes' *Koza Dabasa* by Henry Johnson
Yuming's *The 14th Moon* by Lasse Lehtonen

Forthcoming Titles:
Yellow Magic Orchestra's *Yellow Magic Orchestra* by Toshiyuki Ohwada
Kohaku Utagassen: The Red and White Song Contest by Shelley Brunt

## 33 1/3 Brazil

Series Editor: Jason Stanyek

Covering the genres of samba, tropicália, rock, hip hop, forró, bossa nova, heavy metal and funk, among others, **33 1/3 Brazil** is a series devoted to in-depth examination of the most important Brazilian albums of the twentieth and twenty-first centuries.

Published Titles:
Caetano Veloso's *A Foreign Sound* by Barbara Browning
Tim Maia's *Tim Maia Racional Vols. 1 &2* by Allen Thayer
João Gilberto and Stan Getz's *Getz/Gilberto* by Brian McCann
Gilberto Gil's *Refazenda* by Marc A. Hertzman
Dona Ivone Lara's *Sorriso Negro* by Mila Burns
Milton Nascimento and Lô Borges's *The Corner Club*
    by Jonathon Grasse
Racionais MCs' *Sobrevivendo no Inferno* by Derek Pardue
Naná Vasconcelos's *Saudades* by Daniel B. Sharp
Chico Buarque's First *Chico Buarque* by Charles A. Perrone

Forthcoming titles:
Jorge Ben Jor's *África Brasil* by Frederick J. Moehn

## 33 1/3 Europe
Series Editor: Fabian Holt
Spanning a range of artists and genres, **33 1/3 Europe** offers engaging accounts of popular and culturally significant albums of Continental Europe and the North Atlantic from the twentieth and twenty-first centuries.

Published Titles:
Darkthrone's *A Blaze in the Northern Sky* by Ross Hagen
Ivo Papazov's *Balkanology* by Carol Silverman
Heiner Müller and Heiner Goebbels's *Wolokolamsker Chaussee*
    byPhilip V. Bohlman
Modeselektor's *Happy Birthday!* by Sean Nye
Mercyful Fate's *Don't Break the Oath* by Henrik Marstal
Bea Playa's *I'll Be Your Plaything* by Anna Szemere and András Rónai
Various Artists' *DJs do Guetto* by Richard Elliott
Czesław Niemen's *Niemen Enigmatic* by Ewa Mazierska and
    Mariusz Gradowski
Massada's *Astaganaga* by Lutgard Mutsaers

Los Rodriguez's *Sin Documentos* by Fernán del Val and Héctor Fouce
Édith Piaf's *Récital 1961* by David Looseley
Nuovo Canzoniere Italiano's *Bella Ciao* by Jacopo Tomatis
Iannis Xenakis' *Persepolis* by Aram Yardumian

Forthcoming Titles:
Amália Rodrigues's *Amália at the Olympia* by Lila Ellen Gray
Ardit Gjebrea's *Projekt Jon* by Nicholas Tochka
Vopli Vidopliassova's *Tantsi* by Maria Sonevytsky

**33 1/3 Oceania**
Series Editors: Jon Stratton (senior editor) and Jon Dale (specializing in books on albums from Aotearoa/New Zealand)
Spanning a range of artists and genres from Australian Indigenous artists to Maori and Pasifika artists, from Aotearoa/New Zealand noise music to Australian rock, and including music from Papua and other Pacific islands, **33 1/3 Oceania** offers exciting accounts of albums that illustrate the wide range of music made in the Oceania region.

Published Titles:
John Farnham's *Whispering Jack* by Graeme Turner
The Church's *Starfish* by Chris Gibson
Regurgitator's *Unit* by Lachlan Goold and Lauren Istvandity
Kylie Minogue's *Kylie* by Adrian Renzo and Liz Giuffre
Alastair Riddell's *Space Waltz* by Ian Chapman
Hunters and Collectors's *Human Frailty* by Jon Stratton

Forthcoming Titles:
Ed Kuepper's *Honey Steel's Gold* by John Encarnacao
The Dead C's *Clyma est mort* by Darren Jorgensen
Chain's *Toward the Blues* by Peter Beilharz
Bic Runga's *Drive* by Henry Johnson
The Front Lawn's *Songs from the Front Lawn* by Matthew Bannister
Hilltop Hoods' *The Calling* by Dianne Rodger
Screamfeeder's *Kitten Licks* by Ben Green and Ian Rogers
Luke Rowell's *Buy Now* by Michael Brown

# Human Frailty

Jon Stratton

BLOOMSBURY ACADEMIC
NEW YORK • LONDON • OXFORD • NEW DELHI • SYDNEY

BLOOMSBURY ACADEMIC
Bloomsbury Publishing Inc
1385 Broadway, New York, NY 10018, USA
50 Bedford Square, London, WC1B 3DP, UK
29 Earlsfort Terrace, Dublin 2, Ireland

BLOOMSBURY, BLOOMSBURY ACADEMIC and the Diana logo are
trademarks of Bloomsbury Publishing Plc

First published in the United States of America 2023

A catalog record for this book is available from Library of Congress.

ISBN: HB: 978-1-5013-9785-1
PB: 978-1-5013-9784-4
ePDF: 978-1-5013-9787-5
eBook: 978-1-5013-9786-8

Typeset by Deanta Global Publishing Services, Chennai, India
Printed and bound in Great Britain

Series: 33 ⅓ Oceania

To find out more about our authors and books visit www.bloomsbury
.com and sign up for our newsletters.

# Contents

# Acknowledgements

Big thanks to Peter Beilharz and to Jon Dale both of whom read and commented on earlier versions of this book. Special thanks to Panizza Allmark for her support during the writing of this book and for her critical reading of it. Thanks go to UniSA Creative and Professor Susan Luckman, Director of the research centre Creative People, Products and Places, for providing funds to aid the publication of this book. Thanks to Mar Bucknell for his copyediting and indexing work. Thanks also to Jess Taylor who worked so hard and so well on the book's references and formatting.

# Introduction
## Where it all began

I saw Hunters and Collectors in early August 1986 when they were touring in promotion of the *Human Frailty* album, which had been released at the beginning of April. The gig was held in the refectory at the Student Union facilities of the University of Queensland. The room was packed with a mostly, but by no means completely, male audience. The sound was massive and I was taken aback by the brass section, the Horns of Contempt as they were known. I knew they were a part of the band but I had not expected them to be so integrated into the overall sound and so much a part of the band's driving beat. It was a winter evening in Brisbane and so relatively cool but the room was literally dripping with sweat. The audience, inevitably clearly mostly students, was increasingly drunk and the room heaved as they swayed to the pounding energy of the music. I had been in Australia for four years and been to many gigs but this was my first experience of pub rock, as it became known. In England I had been to gigs by rock groups and punk groups, in pubs, in halls at universities and at festivals, among other venues, but I had never experienced anything quite like this mass, drunken homosociality – the sense of inclusion of audience with the band that was happening at that gig. This reached a high point during 'Say Goodbye', the first track on

*Human Frailty*, when Mark Seymour, as the song's protagonist, quotes his girlfriend ending the affair by stating, 'You don't make me feel like a woman anymore' – and it seemed like the entire audience joined in. I was flabbergasted, not just at the communal singing in the gig but at what was being sung.

In 1986 Queensland was still under the heel of Joh Bjelke-Petersen. Joh had become premier in 1968 and did not leave office until forced out as the result of the Fitzgerald inquiry into corruption in December 1987. Under Joh, Queensland was the most conservative and repressive state in Australia, rivalled only by Western Australia. The police operated as the enforcing arm of the government. Punk and some other genres of popular music were viewed as subversive and gigs were often heavily policed and sometimes broken up. As we drove away from the Hunters and Collectors gig the police were waiting at the roundabout that marked the beginning of Sir Fred Schonell Drive and the entry to the university. Cars were being stopped and checked for drugs and drivers breathalysed. After the strange liberation of the gig this harassment was a return to everyday life in Queensland in the 1980s.

\*   \*   \*

*Human Frailty* was a pivotal album for Hunters and Collectors. It marked their move from being a hip, inner-city Melbourne band with a sound founded in white funk and influenced by the Germanic tradition known as Krautrock to playing a more straight-ahead rock music of the type known as Oz Rock. *Human Frailty* melded both forms of music into a sound which took the best from both traditions. It was produced by the Englishman, Gavin MacKillop. In 1985 MacKillop had produced the Australian group Do-Re-Mi's first album *Domestic Harmony* in London and Deborah Conway, the group's lead singer, recommended him to Hunters and Collectors. Seymour said at the time that MacKillop had 'wanted to make an organic album', by which we can understand an album which had a unified quality rather than feeling like a collection of disparate tracks, and that he wanted the album to be 'a record based on how we play . . . with music based on rhythm' (Sly 1986). Rhythm is here a code for the importance of the drums and bass in Hunters and Collectors' sonic palette.

Also in 1986 MacKillop produced the English group Shriekback's album *Big Night Music*. This album was similarly pivotal in Shriekback's career moving them from avant-garde post-punk to a more accessible pop sound. The critic Bill Cassel (undated (a)) remarks: '*Big Night Music* continued Shriekback's evolution from fringe weirdoes to unlikely pop stars'. It is surely not coincidental that the term 'human frailty' is used in the liner notes to *Big Night Music*: 'Seductive though they are, Shriekback have opted to make a different kind of music – one which exalts human frailty and the harmonious mess of nature over the simplistic reductions of our crude computers' (Cassel undated (a)). If we think of this in connection with the Hunters and Collectors album, it suggests a new emphasis for Shriekback on the kinds of human qualities privileged by Hunters and Collectors. Including *Domestic Harmony*, what all three albums have in common is a white funk influence.

There are deeper connections between Shriekback and early Hunters and Collectors. Hunters and Collectors' first recordings have been compared by critics to those of Gang of Four. For example, in a December 1983 review in the American music paper *Cashbox* of a gig they performed in Los Angeles, George Koulermos (1983) writes: 'Songs like "Talking To A Stranger" and "Towtruck," with fragmented, nonsensical lyrics and early Gang of Four bass licks coupled with sharp guitar attacks were the show's highlights' and in an *AllMusic* review of the band's first album Bill Cassel (undated (b)) adds Shriekback to the comparison, describing the self-titled first Hunters and Collectors album as 'seething art funk comparable to a harder-edged Shriekback or less political Gang of Four'. Dave Allen, one of the founders of Shriekback, had played bass with Gang of Four. Mike Howlett, who produced Hunters and Collectors' *Payload* EP in 1982 produced *Songs of the Free* for Gang of Four in the same year, their first album after Allen had left. MacKillop succeeded in making the white funk influence of such bands acceptable to audiences brought up on the more straight-ahead sounds of pop and rock. Reflecting this accessibility, in Australia *Domestic Harmony* reached number 6 on the album chart and *Human Frailty* number 10 the following year.

The quality of *Human Frailty* was recognized quickly in Australia's mainstream music awards. In 1986 *Human Frailty* was nominated for best album alongside Paul Kelly's *Gossip* and Crowded House's self-titled album in the last Countdown awards, run by the ABC (Australian Broadcasting Corporation) television music program of the same name. John Farnham's *Whispering Jack* won. In 1987 *Human Frailty* was nominated for best album in the first ARIA (Australian Recording Industry Association) awards only for Farnham's more musically pop-oriented album to win again. In the same awards, 'Say Goodbye' from the album, which climbed to number 24 on the singles chart in 1986, was nominated for the year's best single. The remarkable video for 'Everything's On Fire', which was also released as a single and got to number 78 on the singles chart, directed by Andrew de Groot who in that same year, 1986, worked as the cinematographer on Richard Lowenstein's film *Dogs in Space*, was nominated for Best Video. Earlier, in 1982, Lowenstein had made the ground-breaking video for Hunters and Collectors' single, 'Talking To A Stranger'.

Hunters and Collectors formed around late 1980 and early 1981. Their first gig, at the Seaview Ballroom in St Kilda, was on 15 May 1981. The core members, John Archer who played bass, Doug Falconer, the drummer, Robert Miles, best described as the sound engineer, and Mark Seymour, the singer and guitarist, had all been members of a Melbourne University group called the Jetsonnes. The singer of that group was Margot O'Neill who went on to a high-profile career in journalism working for the ABC on both radio and television.

The only member of the Jetsonnes, and subsequently Hunters and Collectors, who was not studying for a degree at Melbourne University was Ray Tosti-Guerra. The guitarist played in his father's cabaret band. John Archer studied Engineering, Doug Falconer Medicine, Robert Miles Architecture and Mark Seymour has an Arts degree. Geoff Crosby, who was a founding member of Hunters and Collectors playing keyboards and synthesizer, had a degree in Architecture from the University of Melbourne and had gone on to take a BA in Painting from Caulfield Institute of Technology. Crosby and Seymour had started writing songs together in December 1980. The brass players were just as highly qualified. Jack Howard, the trumpet player, had a music degree from La Trobe University and had played with the Melbourne Youth Orchestra and Jeremy Smith, who joined Hunters and Collectors to play the French horn, had dropped out of Medicine and played with the Melbourne Symphony Orchestra. Michael Waters, who played trombone, had a Commerce degree from University of Melbourne.

That the band was mostly composed of highly qualified players may seem extraordinary. However, John Clifforth (2020: 28), who studied Medicine at the University of Melbourne during the late 1970s and early 1980s, writing about the inner-city scene at the time, remarks that

> there was this sense of growth, coming out of the kind of anarchy that was going on at University of Melbourne at the time. There was a transition from the hippie dinosaur bands culture of that period to younger kids looking for something completely new.

The Melbourne inner-city scene of the time included a large number of undergraduates. Clifforth himself went on to be a member of Deckchairs Overboard along with Paul Hester who had drummed for International Exiles and who would later play in the last incarnation of Split Enz and then in Crowded House. Deckchairs Overboard's self-titled album, their only one, reached number 88 on the Australian album chart in 1985.

The most enigmatic member of Hunters and Collectors from a historical point of view was Greg Perano. In his memoir of the band *Thirteen Tonne Theory*, Seymour (2009: 5) introduces him in a kind of preface to the beginning of Hunters and Collectors as a mythical figure playing guitar in a squat to a bevy of punk girls:

> There was this one Maori-looking bloke who used to stand in the middle of the room topless, playing a green Hernandez electric guitar through a Fender amp that lay on the floor at his feet. He also had a vacuum cleaner that he turned on, aiming the hose with his right hand at the middle pick-up.

Seymour writes that after the place was raided and the girls stopped coming Perano moved to London. Perano went to London in 1980 so the scene Seymour describes must be earlier. We next meet him when Seymour invites him to join the new band he is putting together. The vignette is centred on Seymour helping Perano extract an old hot-water cylinder from the undergrowth in the yard of the house that he had played in before he went to London. That hot-water cylinder, hit with a glockenspiel key, became Perano's most important instrument during his time with Hunters and Collectors (Seymour 2009: 25–9).

In Chris Bourke's book about Crowded House he tells us that Perano got to know Nick and Mark Seymour through the Boys Next Door scene. In that book Perano explains:

> You're talking about a group of 150 core people, you met them all pretty quickly. Nick was very much a part of it, Mark was still on the outskirts. He was a bit of dag then really, being a schoolteacher. But he had a good feeling about him because he was really obsessed about playing music. Mark's first group, the Jetsonnes, were a very good pop band but they didn't fit in. It was a tight little scene. (Bourke 1997: 37)

The Boys Next Door included Nick Cave and in 1980, after they went to London, subsequently mutated into the Birthday Party. Nick Seymour, Mark's younger brother, later joined Neil Finn, becoming the bass player in Crowded House from late 1984. The scene Perano is talking about became known as the little band scene. This ran from 1979 to 1981. In a detailed description on Wikipedia (2022) the little band scene is described as 'an experimental post-punk scene' which was 'instigated by groups Primitive Calculators and Whirlywhirld'. Perano has described it:

> You'd put a little band together for the night and go on for 10 minutes. There would be complete cacophony of sound, but it was always entertaining. I had a band called Anne's Dance Marathon Band. We used to tape Hitler's speeches and church bells and horses galloping. I'd play the guitar with a teaspoon and smash glass on it, we'd have percussion, sax and violin – it used to drive people out of the room. . . . this was 1979. (Bourke 1997: 38)

This was around the time Seymour describes Perano playing guitar and vacuum cleaner in the squat.

Perano formed a band called True Wheels with John Clifforth. He explains:

> I played Greg some tunes I'd written and he said 'let's form a band' and we formed True Wheels. We classed ourselves as New Wave – via *Talking Heads '77*, Jonathan Richman and that sort of style. We covered Eno's 'Baby's on Fire', songs like that as well as our own material. . . . We used to play gigs with the Boys Next Door, play at Universities, union nights, little clubs, a corner in a pub, places like that. (Clifforth 2020: 28–9)

True Wheels were no doubt named after the Eno track 'The True Wheel' on Eno's *Taking Tiger Mountain (by Strategy)* album released in 1974. Later, it was Perano who named Hunters and Collectors after a track on the Krautrock group Can's album, *Landed*, released in 1975. Clifforth (2020: 29) has a much less grand take on the little band scene, simply calling the short-term groupings 'impromptu bands'.

It would seem, then, that Perano was more deeply embedded in the Melbourne inner-city scene than Mark Seymour and the rest of the Jetsonnes. Nevertheless, a common feature was the white funk influence of Talking Heads. Talking Heads toured Australia in June 1979 and played Melbourne's Dallas Brooks Hall. This was the same year that the small band scene started. At the gig, Phillip Taylor (undated) remembers:

> Ross [elder brother] pointing out a ramshackle bunch of blokes who he identified as local band The Boys Next Door. The defining moment of the night came during 'Psycho Killer', when a heavy booted punk strode up the centre aisle and plunged a large hunting knife into the floorboards of the stage. David Byrne, who at that stage of his career was a far shyer performer than the big-suited extrovert the world would later come to know. Up until that point he had barely ventured toward the front of the stage, and he beat an immediate retreat to the relative safety of the drum kit [syntax as in original].

Both Jack Howard and Mark Seymour were at the gig though as yet they did not know each other. In Howard's (2020: 24) telling:

> There was no light show, all of the house lights were up and they played all of those killer songs. It was a riveting performance

but during 'Psycho Killer', a young dude approached the stage in a trench coat, pulled out a long carving knife and stabbed it quivering into the floor at David Byrne's feet. It was a scary and confronting moment that rattled the band and the crowd. Very punk.

It turns out that the punk in question was a member of the group that included Seymour. His name was James. Seymour (2009: 11) adds that as he stuck the knife into the stage: 'His hand slipped down over the guard and drove the cutting edge deep into the flesh of his palm. Blood sprayed out across the boards at Byrne's feet'. When James was asked why he had done this, he replied: 'For fuck's sake, isn't it obvious? They were so fucking BORING!' (Seymour 2009: 12). It would seem that many of those in the Melbourne inner-city scene went to the Talking Heads gig.

Talking Heads were a touchstone for the local white funksters. James's reaction suggests the extent to which the Melbourne funk sound, with its admixture of punk, was becoming much harder, a development epitomized in the music of Hunters and Collectors a year or so later. The Jetsonnes only recorded one track. 'Newspaper' was released in 1980 on a give-away single with a track by International Exiles, 'Miniskirts in Moscow', on the other side. 'Newspaper' bears a resemblance to Talking Heads' 'Life During Wartime' off their 1979 *Fear of Music* album, an album which, incidentally, had been produced by Eno.

Perano had become friendly with Nick Seymour. When he returned from London he talked with Nick about the music he had heard there: 'Greg had all these ideas, African sounding percussion grooves using electronics, bands like Aswad, Pigbag, Shriekback' (Bourke 1997: 38). The inclusion of Aswad, a

London-based group made up of the sons of Caribbean migrants, in the list signals the influence of reggae for Perano. When Perano returns to London with Hunters and Collectors in 1983 he is asked by Immigration what kind of music the band plays. He answers: 'Reggae funk fusion with rock roots and a tinge of New York underground in the guitars' (Seymour 2009: 80). This sums up well Perano's own influences at this time. Nick's memory is a little awry here as Pigbag formed in late 1980 and Shriekback in 1981, however, white funk in groups like Gang of Four, Level 42, and A Certain Ratio (also named after a line in Eno's 'The True Wheel') was a common aspect of the UK indie scene by the end of 1980.

In 1987 Simon Reynolds commented on the evolution of white funk: 'Funk Flesh + Punk Attitude: this was the fantasy that possessed the rock intelligentsia in the early Eighties. . . . [Bands like] (Talking Heads, Cabaret Voltaire, 23 Skidoo, A Certain Ratio) staged a remotivation of funk, replacing its extrovert upfullness with art rock concerns: alienation, breakdown, psychosis'. Reynolds sums up 'avant-funk enacts a theatre of psychosis' (1987). Perhaps no band illustrates this argument better than Hunters and Collectors during the period before *Human Frailty*. In a 1982 interview Perano was asked if the band plays 'White funk like the early Gang of Four and A Certain Ratio'. He replies: 'Yeah, but I don't like Gang of Four very much. I don't really relate to what they do' (Delaney 1982). Perano references The Pop Group and James Brown as influences.

Nick Seymour provides this version of the beginnings of Hunters and Collectors:

I convinced my brother Mark, who had a band called the Jetsonnes, to form a band with Greg, myself, and a friend of ours, Geoff Crosby. Within about two months Mark and I had a falling out – as brothers do – and he went back to the Jetsonnes with Greg and Geoff and formed Hunters and Collectors. Their first shows – basically, the first two Hunters albums – had that energy borrowed from the UK. Hypnotic, trance-like rhythms, created from electronic and percussion instruments, with a bit of bushman thrown in for good measure (Bourke 1997: 38).

These were the albums that included Perano's percussive funk. Here we can see the connection with Mark Seymour's story about Perano's hot-water cylinder.

By the time of *Human Frailty* Perano was no longer in the band. When Seymour writes the story of Perano being forced out, he focuses it on his feelings of being in competition with Perano for influence in Hunters and Collectors. However, what he also reveals is that he had not been talking to Perano for a year before Perano's exit. The pivotal event happened in London. Some of the band had gone to the pub for a drink. Returning, and passing Perano's room,

> with a drunk man's courage I stuck my head inside and told him to turn the music down. It was 'Holland Tunnel Dive' . . . AGAIN! As we filed into the TV room at the back, with me at the back of the line, he cornered me in the doorway, grabbed me by the shirt front, lifted me clear of the floor and told me to get out of his 'fucking face, you weak little cunt' (Seymour 2009: 141).

For Seymour this was the final straw. However, the battle with Perano was really about musical style.

The funk in Hunters and Collectors sound came from Perano's influence. After he left, the band became more rock-orientated and Seymour's interest in melody moved increasingly to the fore. The key here is understanding 'Holland Tunnel Dive'. The track is by impLOG, a project of Don Christensen. Christensen, an avant-garde artist based in New York, played drums for James Chance's band The Contortions on the 1979 album *Buy* and for Chance's other incarnation as James White and the Blacks on the album *Off White* released the same year. Chance's work can be characterized as white funk or avant-funk, but much harder and more difficult to appreciate than the more pop-oriented work of Talking Heads. Christensen went on to a lengthy collaboration with the minimalist composer Philip Glass.

The listing for 'Holland Tunnel Dive' on the Dark Entries Records site (undated) has this description of Christensen: 'He began making music using found sounds, a Univox drum machine, guitar stomp boxes, Casio keyboards and percussion instruments'. This suggests similar preoccupations to Perano when he was performing on the little band scene. The same site has a description of 'Holland Tunnel Dive':

'Holland Tunnel Dive' is a monotone lament, with a narrator reciting all that is missing in his life along to a sparse, mechanical beat. A variable speed Milwaukee drill creeps its way into the song, eventually reaching cacophonous levels. After four minutes of industrial motorik, an upbeat saxophone riff breaks out unexpectedly, unsettling the listener even further. (Dark Entries Records undated)

This is not Seymour's taste in music but in its anarchic quality resembles Hunters and Collectors' initial performances. In his review of *Thirteen Tonne Theory*, Jack Marx (2008) reminisces:

Few who saw the group in those early years will easily forget the encounter. They were awesome, tribal and ethereal, their stage decked in skulls under canopies and jungle netting, the whole experience, like the Morlock sirens in H G Wells' *The Time Machine*, entrancing the audience into some bizarre world of subterranean cannibalism.

He adds: 'It was post-punk theatre at its most stylised and spectacular' (Marx 2008). Marx comments that all this had been lost when the band returned from their abortive London trip, that visit where Seymour had his confrontation with Perano.

The musical form of 'Holland Tunnel Dive' bears a similarity to some of the work on the second Hunters and Collectors album, *The Fireman's Curse*. This album was the one most influenced by Perano's ideas. Here is part of Rho-X's description:

> The industrial epic funk-rock 'The Fireman's Curse' brings to mind a fusion between the Simple Minds and Cabaret Voltaire, while the grotesque industrial music-hall 'Fish Roar' brings to mind Foetus' orgies. 'Blind Snake Sundae' veers into atmospherics and utilizes a more minimal approach, although the tortured wails of the singer echo Nick Cave and The Pop Group at their most desperate. . . . 'Slave, Moan & Sway' shows how they can build an elaborate, multi-layered industrial-funk, until they reach a genuinely menacing atmosphere; this isn't dissimilar at all to how Shriekback and Yello operate. (2018)

We should note particularly the reference to Shriekback here and remember that band's connection with *Human Frailty*. As we shall see in Chapter 3, while in London Seymour was listening to quite different music, Van Morrison's 1968 release, *Astral Weeks*. This is an album of gorgeous jazz-inflected melodies.

It was Perano who brought the funk to Hunters and Collectors and he thought of the band's music in terms of jamming, where the jam of so many musicians together built the funk. In a 1982 interview where he references James Brown, Perano discusses the band's practice like this:

> We try to work on that strong rhythmic undercurrent which people seem to interpret as funk, but it's influenced by a variety of different things. We're a fairly traditional band, really. We work and write together as a group. We work off each other which is probably the way the best bands work. We all contribute to what's going on. (Delaney 2014)

Seymour increasingly saw this communal ethic as stifling his art. The confrontation with Perano was about two views for the musical direction of Hunters and Collectors; communal or with individual leadership, funk or melodic rock, hipster credibility or mainstream success. In *Thirteen Tonne Theory* Seymour (2009: 139) explains the differences in approach:

> The idea that you could build a repertoire based solely on 'jamming' was Perano's. It was a romantic notion that allowed the band's egalitarian culture to flourish – and one that I grew to hate.

Seymour won the battle. Perano went on to form The Deadly Hume, a group which continued some of the ideas in *The Fireman's Curse*. Hunters and Collectors' next album, *The Jaws of Life*, marked the beginning of a transition in which *Human Frailty* was most pivotal. At the same time, much was lost as the communal jamming and the funk disappeared out of the band's music. This is most obvious in the albums after *Human Frailty*. Seymour (2009: 142) remarks that in forcing Perano out of the band he 'won something. But to this day I'm not sure exactly what it was'. Perhaps this is because what was lost was at least as important as what was won.

# **1** Apocalyptic visions and road stories

*Human Frailty* comes between the apocalyptic lyrical concerns of the earlier songs and the often more directly personal and political concerns of the lyrics of the band's later songs. It is an album of rock songs where there remains a hint of funk in many of the tracks. At the same time it is an exception in the band's catalogue. It is an album founded on desire, love, lust, loss and guilt. It is the band's most personal album, lyrically charting Mark Seymour's love affair with a woman he names elsewhere as May. From this perspective the intensity of the songs on *Human Frailty* can be heard as a reaction to the apocalyptic preoccupations which weave through much of the earlier material. The relationship addressed on *Human Frailty* can be understood as a haven from a world coming apart. This chapter discusses the apocalyptic themes of Hunters and Collectors' earlier material, placing them in the context of the Australian experience of the early 1980s.

Hunters and Collectors formed in late 1980 at the beginning of the decade. In the liner notes to their 2003 *Natural Selection/ Greatest Hits* collection, Seymour (2003) writes:

> The eighties is often looked upon as an insipid, at best, friendly sort of time, when everyone was trying to get rich and Australia

was opening up to the outside world. Hunters and Collectors flourished in that era despite the fact that their songs told a different story.

He adds: 'The optimism of those times seems laughable now.' Optimism is a description often used as a characteristic of the Australian experience in the 1980s.

Frank Bongiorno (2015: x–xi), in his book on Australia in that decade, identifies as familiar elements, 'the optimism, the energy, the elitism (frequently combined with a pretend egalitarianism), the excess and the crash'. The specific crash to which he is referring here is that of Mike Gore, the developer who built the Sanctuary Cove gated community on an island off Queensland's Gold Coast. Gore subsequently left for Canada owing around $25 million. Gore's fate was shared by many of the entrepreneurs of the 1980s.

The 1980s were a time of incredible transition in Australia. Bongiorno (2015: xi) offers two alternative views of the decade:

> The journalist Paul Kelly famously claimed that the eighties saw the end of the Australian Settlement, the suite of ideas and policies that had underpinned the nation from the early twentieth century. White Australia, Industry Protection, Wage Arbitration, State Paternalism and Imperial Benevolence: all, said Kelly, were broken by the end of the 1980s . . . But another journalist, George Megalogenis, saw the eighties less as an end than as a beginning, a prelude to 'The Australian Moment', his name for the vindication of twenty-five years of policy reform that came with the economy's astonishing resilience during the global financial crisis of 2008.

The decade was both these things, the end of the old Australia epitomized in the seventeen-year post-war conservative prime ministership of Robert Menzies and the beginning of a new Australia that was centred on the opening up of the country to the world; the new diversity of migrants after the ending of the White Australia policy; the floating of the Australian dollar; and the ending of trade protectionism. Much of this was carried out through the charismatic leadership of the Labor prime minister Bob Hawke, from 1983, and his svelte Treasurer, Paul Keating. Conservatives saw these developments as threatening and the restructuring of industry following on from the globalization of trading relations meant that many workers lost their employment. We will return to this in the next chapter on Oz Rock. However, many were excited by the changes which offered everything from new industries founded in new technologies to the varied impacts of increasing integration with south-east Asia to a greatly expanded variety of foods brought by the new migrants.

These developments helped provide the basis for the new inner-city arts scenes that flowered in all the major Australian cities from around the mid-1970s. Writing about one particular street in Fitzroy, an inner-city suburb in Melbourne, Seamus O'Hanlon and Simone Sharpe (2009: 293) describe how: 'As clothing, footwear and food production and distribution left, new users moved in, and from the early 1970s sections of the street began to develop a "bohemian" cultural ambience.' Already in decline as signalled here, clothing and footwear were two of the industries that suffered as a consequence of the lowering of trade tariffs by the Hawke government.

O'Hanlon and Sharpe (2009: 290) note the general changes that were happening:

> The transformation of this one street from a site of working-class housing and manufacturing and blue-collar employment before the 1970s to a high-cost, post-industrial address today is … similar to that which has been documented by geographers, sociologists and other social scientists in numerous studies of gentrification and urban renewal in cities in Australia and internationally in recent decades.

Punk, and the arts scene related to it in Australia, was a beneficiary of these developments. Melbourne has a history of artists in the inner city, particularly Carlton, stretching deep into the 1970s. This is the inner-city scene discussed in the Introduction. David Laing with Jewel Brown (2014) explains: 'Underground rock in mid-70s Melbourne was the raw outgrowth of a thriving live music, arts and theatre-based counterculture and a progressive left-wing sensibility coming together with rowdy celebration in the inner northern suburb of Carlton.' This scene was closely linked with students from Melbourne University. This is the scene which produced the Shnorts who transformed into the Jetsonnes and who in 1980 morphed into Hunters and Collectors.

The urban environment which enabled the post-punk scene was magnified by the changes wrought as a consequence of Hawke and Keating's opening up of the domestic economy to foreign competition. As Zora Simic (2020: 110) remarks: 'In Australia, unlike England, the punk scene was a mostly middle-class phenomenon.' Out of this scene in Melbourne came, among other groups, the Boys Next Door and, after they left for London, 'the next big thing' as Hunters and Collectors were called.

While the transformation in the Australian economy, and its impacts on social and cultural life, was experienced by many as unsettling, perceived as either bad or good, there was evolving a development which many settler Australians found far more anxiety producing – the issue of land rights. Indigenous campaigns for land rights began in the 1970s. The New South Wales Aboriginal Land Council was formed in October 1977 and it submitted ten land claims to the state government between 1977 and 1981. The New South Wales government established a Ministry of Aboriginal Affairs in 1981 and a state Aboriginal Land Rights Act was passed in 1983. In that same year, land rights was part of the platform on which the Hawke Labor government was elected. Clyde Holding, the Minister for Aboriginal Affairs, stated five principles of land rights: inalienable freehold title, full legal protection for sacred sites, Aboriginal control over mining on Aboriginal land, access to mining royalty equivalents and compensation for lost land (Korff 2021). Subsequently, in the face of concerted campaigns by mining companies and the Labor state government in Western Australia, federal Labor backed down on land rights legislation. In May 1982, Eddie Mabo and others began a legal case for land rights on the Murray Islands in the Torres Strait. After ten years, in 1992, the case was won. One implication of the case was that the legal fiction that Australia was terra nullius, no one's land, when it was settled was overturned.

Barry Morris (2013: 2) starts his book on the history of the struggle for land rights: 'For a generation of Indigenous men and women, the period from the 1970s to the 1990s was one of unprecedented political agency and legislative change in their struggles for recognition of postcolonial rights.' Through the 1980s Aborigines fought a lengthy public relations campaign for land rights. One example was the employment of the saying 'Always was, always will be Aboriginal land' which was chanted at protest demonstrations and was printed on t-shirts. At the same time the mining lobby, in conjunction with some politicians, ran scare campaigns about the threat posed by land rights.

In 1980 in Western Australia, the premier Charles Court stated:

> The land of Western Australia doesn't belong to the Aborigines. The idea that Aborigines, because of having lived in this land before the days of white settlement have some prior title to lands somehow gives them perpetual right to demand tribute of all others who may inhabit it is not only inconsistent with any idea of fairness or common humanity, in fact it is as crudely selfish and racist a notion as one can imagine. (Riley 1994: 169)

The Liberals lost power in 1983 and in 1984, the leader of the Liberal opposition in Western Australia, Bill Hassell, put his name and photo 'to a party brochure which made the false claim that half the state would be granted to Aboriginal people as a result of the recommendations of the Seaman Land Inquiry' (Riley 1994: 169). The Report of the Aboriginal Land Inquiry, otherwise known as the Seaman Inquiry, which had been established by the new Labor government, recommended that Aborigines should be able to refuse mining on their land. At the same time the Chamber of Mines in Western Australia ran a series of television advertisements asking, for example,

'Can you afford to pay the price of unequal land rights?' The consequence of the divisive publicity campaigns by the mining lobby was a profound unsettling of Australian settler understanding of Australia as home. Indeed, in the wake of the Mabo decision, Jeff Kennett, then premier of Victoria, claimed that 'suburban backyards could be at risk of takeover by Aboriginal people' (Kennedy 2012).

Through the 1980s, and especially during the first half of the decade, one thread of commentary on Hunters and Collectors associated them with Aborigines. In 1982, in an interview in the Aotearoa/New Zealand music magazine *Rip It Up*, Doug Falconer felt it necessary to say, 'We never had aspirations to be an aboriginal-inspired [*sic*] band' (Brown 1982). The following year in a review of a gig in Los Angeles, quoted from earlier, George Koulermos (1983) wrote:

> Hunters and Collectors' savage brand of music is a form of aboriginal [*sic*] funk incorporating a wide range of styles from the westernised to the tribal rhythms of its own outback and exotic Africa. 'Tribal' seems to be a very accurate adjective to describe what actually goes on at a Hunters show.

The funk of early Hunters and Collectors music was identified not with influences like Talking Heads but with some fantasy about Indigenous Australians. As late as 1986, in an interview related to *Human Frailty*, Seymour was asked about the Aboriginal funk in the band's music to which he replied:

> Americans really wanted to believe that there was some special purity about Australian bands because 'we're in touch with the earth'. We kept on saying, 'We're just middle-class boys from

the suburbs'. I've never had contact with Aborigines. But I think there is a strong sense of landscape in our music. (Sly 1986)

In part this identification was a consequence of the band's early stage presentation described in the previous chapter. Seymour's denial of any connection with Aborigines belies the general feeling of disturbance at the new visibility of Aborigines and Torres Strait Islanders in the settler experience during the 1980s. It is understandable that even the band's name should evoke such an association. While it comes from a Can track, the term echoes the description of Aborigines before white incursion as hunters and gatherers.

Funk has a history in African-American music. James Brown's group had a brass section though one made up rather differently from Hunters and Collectors' Horns of Contempt. Simon Reynolds (1996) has pointed out the influence of James Brown's funk on Can. At the heart of the connections that were made between Hunters and Collectors, African-American funk, the tribal and Aborigines, was a sense of Otherness, that the band was tapping into some characteristic of Australianness that was at once typifyingly Australian but simultaneously disturbing. In a review of a Hunters and Collectors gig from 1981 Craig N. Pearce commented:

At once wanting and disputing the value of tension in their music, it seems as if the perfect sound for the band is one which comes out smooth and controlled yet has that ol' heart of darkness about it. More than one person has commented on how 'black' the sound seems. True – sometimes dangerous, sometimes threatening.

Indeed, in the 1980s, with the impact of the new visibility of Aborigines on urban, white society and the simultaneous debates about land ownership, what was typifyingly Australian was precisely a feeling of unease, of home as being uncanny.

The uncanny is closely aligned with apocalypse. 'Talking To A Stranger' was Hunters and Collectors' first single, released six months after the *World of Stone* EP in July 1982. Seymour's lyrics start with a quotation from Charles Baudelaire's poem 'The Albatross'. Baudelaire describes how bored sailors would capture the bird and how feeble it now seems on the deck of the boat. Seymour translates the first line and uses it to begin each verse of the song. The lyrics are unsettling. They ask us to 'Remember the panic in its delectable face, when I touched it'. This may refer back to the albatross but might also be a statement about the anxiety in personal connection, the kind of connection that drives *Human Frailty*. The lyrics include a female, eroticized Jesus with black eyes. Chris Johnson (2008) describes the track as being 'taboo and transgressive and about being an outsider'. In his liner notes for the *Natural Selection/Greatest Hits* collection, Seymour (2003) writes that the track is: 'Lofty stuff. Apocalyptic dread. The end was nigh.' In *Thirteen Tonne Theory*, he identifies the stranger as death (Seymour 2009: 40).

The video for the track was made by Richard Lowenstein who went on to make the definitive film of Melbourne's post-punk, inner-city scene *Dogs in Space* in 1986. Seymour (2009: 66) writes about the video's apocalyptic quality:

[W]e were swept up on a visual journey that took us into a wild exotic land where the last vestiges of civilisation were stripped away to reveal a desolate place, a vision of Australia, the robust, brutal landscape worn down even further by some awful cataclysm in the immediate past. The 'stranger' was some mythical beast of the future that roamed the horizon on the edge of the sea, or lurked deep inside the dreamscape of the song.

Lowenstein's video is of a piece with other Australian apocalyptic and post-apocalyptic visions of the early 1980s such as the film *Mad Max*, directed by George Miller and released in 1979, and its sequel, *Mad Max 2*, released in 1981.

Monica Germana and Aris Mousoutzanis (2014: 9) suggest: 'In its association with the liminal and the unrepresentable, the uncanny underpins theoretical readings of the apocalypse, pointing to its complex readings of the present and its ambiguous links with the past and the future.' The beast of Lowenstein's video, the stranger of the song, is a manifestation of the uncanny lurking on the edge of settler Australian experience in a time when Aborigines have returned from terra nullius to claim what was taken from them. In 1998 Ken Gelder and Jane Jacobs made a similar point about the feeling of uncanniness experienced by settler Australians in their book titled *Uncanny Australia*. In the Introduction they write that one concern of the book is with,

> [a] consequence of Aboriginal claims for sacredness which we can note here to turn what seems like 'home' into something else, something less familiar, less settled. This is one meaning of the term 'uncanny'. (Gelder and Jacobs 1998: xiv)

Gelder and Jacobs directly link the Aboriginal assertion of sacredness in the land to settler feelings of uncanny dislocation.

Quoting Sigmund Freud on the uncanny, Germana and Mousoutzanis (2014: 9) argue that 'the apocalypse reproduces a "return of the repressed": in signifying "that class of the frightening which leads back to what is known of old and long familiar"'. They go on to quote Evan Calder Williams from his book *Combined and Uneven Apocalypse*:

> What is revealed is what has been hidden in plain sight all along, previously only caught askance from the corner of our eye: the sudden exposure of what was present but not visible, because it didn't accord with those real structuring forces of a totality. (Germana and Mousoutzanis 2014: 10)

In 1980s Australia what had been hidden and was now revealed were the original inhabitants of the land.

It is in this context that we should think about Hunters and Collectors' first release, 'World Of Stone' on the EP of that name. The track starts with what sounds like clap sticks and a didgeridoo. However, the clap sticks are most probably metal percussion instruments and the didgeridoo is 'a deep, almost sub-sonic synth drone which emanated from the Korg MS20' (Seymour 2003). The synthesizer was played by Geoff Crosby. Seymour (2003) describes the track as: 'Apocalyptic fantasy. *Mad Max*.' The lyrics tell us: 'From deep in the jungle where the monkeys are taught / To leap and fall around / Soft and protected from this world of stone.' What is this world of stone? It is most likely that Seymour took the phrase from the title of a short story by Tadeusz Borowski called in English 'The World of Stone'.

Borowski was Polish. In 1943, when he was twenty-one, he was sent to Auschwitz by the German occupying forces. Because he was not Jewish he was made a kapo, someone who had a supervisory role in the death camp. Borowski's world was dominated by concentration camps. In 1926 the Russians had sent his father to a camp in Karelia, in north-western Russia near the border with Finland, and in 1930 his mother was sent to a gulag in Siberia. Set in decimated post-war Warsaw, Borowski's story is about Tadek who walks each day through the ruins and the impoverished people to pick up his government allowance. He plans, as we are told, 'to write a great, immortal epic, worthy of this unchanging, difficult world, chiseled out of stone' (Borowski 2021). For Gordana Crnkovic (2000: 82): 'The "world of stone" is an "unchanging" world because its violence is not a historical contingency that happens by chance but an immanent consequence of the normalcy itself.' Extreme violence is not an aberration. It is the foundation on which everyday life is built. The violence that founds the death camp is simply masked by a banal, non-violent everyday life that appears to make violence seem the exception rather than the basis of human existence. In this interpretation of Seymour's lyrics we are most likely the monkeys protected from the founding world of violence.

On the cover of *World of Stone* is a photograph of a grotesque, a decorative, very fearsome-looking flying dragon much in the style of a stone frill-necked lizard. It is positioned above the corner of a window. Frill-necked lizards are native to northern Australia. It is not just the desert that is brought into the city here but, as Seymour wrote, the apocalypse. The track can be read as disguising a reference to the Aboriginal genocide by a not-so-obscure reference to the Holocaust. From this point of view, the track itself is uncanny. The genocide that had been hidden in plain sight began to be revealed through the voices of the Aboriginal campaigners for land rights in the 1980s.

In 1982 Hunters and Collectors released the *Payload* EP. It includes the track 'Lumps of Lead'. Here, we are told 'Everybody's pinching their guts / Young lumps of lead, floating on the harbour.' The harbour here is Sydney Harbour. The phrase, pinching one's gut, refers to hunger. It is a term that gave the name to Pinchgut Island, named in a later verse, so called because in 1788 Thomas Hill was sentenced to eight days in irons on the small island living on bread and water as punishment for stealing a biscuit from another convict. The island had previously been called Mat-te-wan-ye in the local Aboriginal language. Now the island and its name were overlain with the violence of the convict settlers. In 1796 a gallows and a gibbet were erected on the island for the execution and display of Francis Morgan who had bludgeoned another convict to death. In 1857 the island was levelled and Fort Denison built on it. It is no wonder, with this history, that, as the lyrics tell us: 'And your eyes, watching this, they begin to cry.' The lyrics refer to that violent, convict colonial time suggesting the present is infected by it. Your eyes begin to cry with the horror of that violent past. What is implied again is the Aboriginal genocide inflicted on the first inhabitants as the violent convict world of the settlers was established.

The sense of apocalypse was founded in the uncanny feeling that home was no longer fully home. This feeling was perhaps most intense outside the cities. Always thought of as strange and harsh, the land itself began to be experienced as uncanny, the site of the breakdown of (settler) civilization. The first two *Mad Max* films are the most obvious expression of this. In another example, this one drawn from actual events, in 1980 a nine-week-old baby called Azaria disappeared while she was on a camping trip with her parents, Michael and Lindy Chamberlain. Their tent was pitched near the base of the rock that is now called Uluru but was then known by its settler name of Ayers Rock, given it in 1873 honouring the Chief Secretary of South Australia, Sir Henry Ayers. In a thesis written in 1994, Suzanne Gibson writes:

> Participating in a journey out and through the landscape of 'the [Northern] Territory' was (and is) a re-enactment of non-Aboriginal Australians' 'pioneering' roots and a confirmation of the emotional bond between white Australia and the landscape. More symbolic still and, according to [Bob] Hodge, the 'Holy Grail' of the Australian outback traveller, is Ayers Rock. (Gibson 1994: 10–11)

The Ayers Rock National Park had been created in 1958. In 1979 the local Anangu people lodged a land claim which included Ayers Rock and in 1983 the Hawke government had decided to hand back management of the Rock to the Anangu. The transfer took place in 1985 after which Ayers Rock became known also by its Indigenous name of Uluru. By 1982 Lindy Chamberlain had been convicted of murdering her daughter and given a life sentence. She was finally released and the case dismissed in 1988 after new evidence that her claim that Azaria had been carried off by a dingo was proved to be correct.

Running through the 1980s the case was a focus for the settler experience of the uncanniness of the outback. Lynn McCredden (2008: 119) describes the reaction to Azaria's disappearance as a national frenzy in which:

> a litany of strange 'facts' and moral opinions, still able to be recited today by many Australians, began to circulate via the media and from person to person: the child had been named 'Azaria', which means 'sacrifice in the desert'; Lindy had been known to dress the baby in black, with connotations of Satanism or witchery for some pundits; the deed had been committed in a strange, even haunted place, Ayers Rock (Uluru), where Aborigines were making what to non-indigenous Australians sounded like wild claims about sacred connections to the country and the Rock.

The Azaria case, especially because the disappearance took place at Ayers Rock/Uluru, was a lightning rod for settler Australians' anxieties about feeling displaced in their homeland. The case stands with the *Mad Max* films as an expression of the intimations of apocalypse felt by settler Australians.

Customized cars and trucks were central to the apocalyptic vision of the *Mad Max* films and by early 1983 Hunters and Collectors were becoming increasingly interested in trucks. Johnson (2008) suggests that this was related to the band's massive amounts of touring across Australia:

> There's road kill around, dead things. Wrecks. Gunshots in yellow signs. Sweat, roos and laughter under burning sun.

Adelaide is 828 kilometres from the West Gate. That's Australia out your window. Hunters and Collectors fetishized the road. It held arcane codes for them, but it also held firm logic - it took them to the people who wanted to hear them play.

Seymour (2003) comments that 'Little Chalkie' on *The Jaws of Life* is about:

Death, again. Road kill. Evidence that the traveller is at the frontier of civilisation. Here there be dragons . . . and the carcasses of kangaroos on the Great Western Highway.

Note the echo of the grotesque on the cover of *World of Stone*. 'Little Chalkie' is another apocalyptic song, this time about driving the Australian outback roads. The roads offered a two-lane blacktop uncertain imposition of settler society across the vast, uncanny landscape connecting towns and cities.

Hunters and Collectors did not engage directly with the Azaria case. However, on 18 August 1983, Douglas Crabbe accelerated his 25-tonne Mack Super-Liner towing one trailer into the bar of The Inland Motel near the base of Ayers Rock/ Uluru. These motels were closed in 1984 and tourists were accommodated at Yulara just outside the national park. Crabbe had unhitched one of the trailers of his road train as if, in his drunken state, he thought that might mitigate the damage he was about to cause. He had been drinking heavily in the motel bar. Around 12:30, drunk, he had become increasingly obnoxious. Crabbe had been refused further service, and had been told to leave. His subsequent action killed five people and seriously injured a further sixteen. Happening again in the vicinity of Ayers Rock/Uluru, the crime took on a mythic quality. Writing about the genre of Australian films that centres on cars, from *The Cars that Ate Paris* (1974) to the *Mad Max* films and *Dead End Drive-In* (1986), Rebecca Johinke (2009: 309) avers that, 'in these dark comic narratives, the crashed car usually signifies individual, cultural and industrial decline, but it also provides the opportunity for heroism and renewal'. The Crabbe narrative has no heroic driver but the murderous action suggests the decline found in those films. It was this, and the minor apocalypse of the invasion and destruction of the apparently safe space of the motel, and all this taking place again at the site so important to both Indigenous and settler Australians, that gives mythic power to the narrative.

Hunters and Collectors called their third album *The Jaws of Life* with reference to the destruction visited by Crabbe. The Jaws of Life is the name given to the instrument used to prise apart wrecks so that drivers and passengers can be extracted. The first track on the album is '42 Wheels' and the lyrics refer directly to Crabbe. They are written in the first person: 'I've got a heavy little number / I've got 42 wheels of pleasure and pain.' In 1984 Hunters and Collectors had gone back to Germany where they had recorded their second album *The Fireman's Curse* with Conny Plank to record their next album. Plank was closely associated with the Krautrock scene and had produced albums for Kraftwerk, Neu! and Harmonia among others. Seymour (2003) has noted: 'Doing the autobahn in a hired Mercedes. 225 kmh. Totally legal. The first Hunters road stories were written then.'

At the beginning of '42 Wheels' there is the sound of a truck starting up. It was recorded in Germany, a yellow tow truck, a 'six-wheel drive MAN recovery vehicle'. Seymour (2009: 145) remarks: 'The Mixer [Robert Miles] ran it through a DAT player and it hammered out front across a sea of heads in every bar and club in Australia for years afterwards.' The band's interest in tow trucks had begun earlier. On the *Payload* EP there is a track called 'Towtruck': 'We bought a yellow towtruck / To drive it round and round our neighbourhood.' It is also the first track on the band's first album. If crashes are related to civilizational decline, then tow trucks are concerned with salvage, the attempt to rescue civilization. In the prescient Peter Carey story 'Crabs', first published in 1972, on which the film *Dead End Drive-In*, directed by Brian Trenchard-Smith, is based, the titular character's brother drives a tow truck amid a society descending into lawless chaos – much like what is happening to society in the first *Mad Max* film. At the end of the story, Crabs, desperate to leave the drive-in which is being used as a kind of concentration camp for unruly youth, turns into a tow truck. He escapes but the city is dark and disappointing. He ends up back at the gates of the drive-in. It would seem Australian society can no longer be redeemed by tow trucks. In *Mad Max 2* tow trucks are used by the villains. The dystopian *Dead End Drive-In*, has Hunters and Collectors' 'Talking To A Stranger' on the soundtrack.

As Seymour makes clear, apocalypse haunts many of Hunters and Collectors' early tracks. What is unclear is what that apocalypse is. Here, I have wanted to suggest that the band's songs related to apocalypse are a consequence of the uncanniness of the white settler experience in the 1980s that was an effect of the land rights movement and the new assertiveness of Indigenous Australians. The secret fear was that the apocalypse of Aboriginal Australia could return as a future apocalypse for settler Australians. Hunters and Collectors turned the focus of their songs to the road, and simultaneously moved away from a funk sound to be more rock-oriented. They moved from being an inner-city dance band to a rock band travelling the roads of Australia playing to suburban and country pub audiences. At the same time, through the 1980s their songs continued to be invested with the uncanniness and associated sense of apocalypse brought about by the impact of the Aboriginal land rights movement on settler Australia. *Human Frailty* was a reaction to the angst and alienation of the 1980s, a decade that seemed on the surface to be so optimistic. *Human Frailty* turned inwards, discussing personal relationships, but the residue of apocalypse remained. With the notable exception of 'Throw Your Arms Around Me', these were primarily stories of domestic apocalypse, failing and failed relationships.

# 2 The inner-city sound, Pub Rock and Oz Rock

In the lead up to the recording of *Human Frailty*, the band made a decision, at the instigation so he says of Seymour, to start making more generally accessible music. In his recollection, after the critical success but commercial failure of *The Jaws of Life*, it was necessary for the band to make a choice, to either break up or consciously make a record that would sell into a larger market. Seymour remembers telling the rest of the band, 'We have to make a commercial record' (Double 2020). In the interview where he recounts this, Seymour goes on to say that he also remembers thinking, 'I wanna write pop songs' (Double 2020). The album they made was *Human Frailty*. Hunters and Collectors are thought of as an Oz Rock band. However, as we have seen, they started as an inner-city band in Melbourne thought by those in the know likely to replace the Boys Next Door, the band which included Nick Cave and Rowland S. Howard, as the most significant local, inner-city Melbourne band when that band moved to London in 1980 and renamed itself the Birthday Party. Both these terms, inner city and Oz Rock need to be interrogated.

Hunters and Collectors began as a version of a white funk band. Over the albums to *Human Frailty*, the band moved towards becoming a rock band. A pivotal moment was the sacking of Perano. As Seymour (2009: 156) writes: 'With Perano gone there was no more funk, no more groove.' Becoming a rock band meant entering the genre of Australian electric-guitar-based music. We must remember that since the 1950s there has been a division in Australian popular music between rock music, at that time called rock 'n' roll, and pop music, the morally acceptable, sweet music played on mainstream radio. The most popular music, perhaps the most successful in Seymour's use of the term, was pop music. This was the music that sold enough copies to enter the charts. In 1981 the singles which sold most copies included 'Stars on 45' by Stars on 45, 'Antmusic' by Adam and the Ants and 'Jealous Guy' by Roxy Music. The highest selling single by an Australian artist was Men at Work's 'Who Can It Be Now?' at number 9. In 1986, when *Human Frailty* was released, the most popular singles included 'Chain Reaction' by Diana Ross, 'Touch Me (I Want Your Body)' by Samantha Fox and 'Stimulation' by Wa Wa Nee. At number 5 this synth-pop song with a disco influence was the highest selling single by an Australian artist that year. Selling predominantly to an older, male audience, rock music has tended to fare better on album charts. In 1981 the second and third top-selling albums in Australia were by Australian Crawl, *Sirocco*, and AC/DC, *Back in Black*. The ninth best-selling album was *Icehouse* by Flowers, a group who combined synth-pop with rock influences, successfully claiming a middle ground between pop and rock audiences. After changing their name to Icehouse the group continued to have success playing synth-pop. In 1986 Jimmy Barnes, the singer with Oz Rock group Cold Chisel, had the third best-selling album with *For the Working Class Man*, and INXS, who like AC/DC had started their career playing in Sydney pubs and similar venues, had the fourteenth best-selling album with *Listen Like Thieves*.

When Seymour describes the songs on *Human Frailty* as pop he is thinking of the group's movement from having an inner-city cult following to having a much larger, and more national, rock audience. Hunters and Collectors were not the only group to make this shift. The Angels began in Adelaide in 1970 as the Moonshine Jug and String Band. They played on university campuses and cafes. They are best described at this point as an inner-city band. Rick Brewster, who played washboard and shifted to lead guitar, has remembered: 'There was a cult following with The Jug Band but if we wanted any real success we had to start an electric band' (O 2014). In *The Mayor's a Square*, Shane Homan (2003) has an interview with Chris Bailey, The Angels' bass player. He describes how, having gone bankrupt for the second time, the band were looking for a sound that would be popular, provide the success they wanted and indeed needed, if they were to survive as a group. By this time they were playing revivalist rock 'n' roll and had changed their name to the Keystone Angels. In early 1976 they had relocated to Sydney. They were in a rehearsal room in Balmain:

> That's when somebody started playing that full on sound, and Doc [Neeson] added some vocals, and we thought we might be on to something. I told [drummer] Buzz [Bidstrup] to play just four-on-the-floor, and I started thumping just one note – forget the nice bass lines I was playing in country music, and turned [the amplifier] up to ten. (Homan 2003: 192–3)

We should note here the reference to volume. The importance of volume to Oz Rock will be discussed later in this chapter. Releasing their first album in 1977, The Angels went on to be a key Oz Rock act and a mainstay of the pub rock scene.

Unlike The Angels, Cold Chisel were always a pub act. In their early days in Adelaide and when they moved to Melbourne in 1976 and then to Sydney, Cold Chisel were playing mostly covers of songs by artists like English hard rock groups Free, Led Zeppelin and Deep Purple. Success came in 1978 when the group started playing the melodic rock songs written by their keyboard player Don Walker. The first, self-titled, album includes 'Khe Sanh', about a traumatized Vietnam War veteran, which has become an Australian sing-along classic. Anthems were a characteristic of Oz Rock. This album marks Cold Chisel's movement into that genre.

We must work through the sometimes confusing usages of the terms inner-city rock, Oz Rock and pub rock. All three terms refer to music made in Australia roughly between the early 1970s and the late 1980s or early 1990s. A part of the problem with relating the use of the terms to dates is that the music identified by these terms developed at slightly different times in different Australian cities, most specifically Melbourne and Sydney. The term for which there is most consensus is inner-city rock. This refers to a form of music that evolved in the first instance in Melbourne. Perhaps the first use of a permutation of the term was by Clinton Walker in his book *Inner City Sound* published in 1981. This was a polemical book in which Walker championed the music of many of these bands who had evolved in the inner city of Melbourne, and to some extent Sydney and Brisbane. Walker set up an opposition between what he called Oz-Rock and the inner-city sound. In the 2005 Preface to the republished book Walker writes that, 'there is a solid intellectual basis to *Inner City Sound* – that punk reinvented a future for rock, and that Australia hadn't got the credit for its role in that process' (Walker 2005 [1981]: 5). This dates the evolution of inner-city rock to the late 1970s. In the Introduction to the first edition, Walker explains: 'Australian punk/post-punk music is a vital and important force that hasn't been allowed to, but could and should dominate the charts and hearts around the country' (Walker 2005 [1981]: 7). For Walker, the music critic, if only the inner-city music could get generally better known, it would become the music of choice for the majority of Australian young people.

What Walker thought was suffocating the new music that he was writing about was Oz-Rock and the industry apparatus which supported it, most specifically the record company Mushroom that had been started by Michael Gudinski. Walker (2005 [1981]: 8) writes with understandable caution, at the time not identifying Gudinski: 'The Oz-rock establishment rejects the Inner City Sound, probably because to them, it is without commercial potential.' He explains:

> The Inner City Sound is, at least, one of commitment and passion, intelligence, individuality and innovation – and integrity. And if it ever seems at all inaccessible that's only because it's not exactly what the Oz-rock establishment has taught is accessible. (Walker 2005 [1981]: 8)

The implication here is that Oz Rock is stultifying and commercial, lacking in authenticity.

Walker's book is chronological. It begins in 1976–7 discussing among other bands The Saints from Brisbane, Radio Birdman from Sydney and the Boys Next Door from Melbourne. The book originally finished in 1981 when Walker writes about artists including Equal Local, the Go-Betweens and the Sunnyboys, from Melbourne, Brisbane and Sydney, respectively. The 2005 edition includes a further chapter of material written by Walker in the early 1980s, after the publication of the first edition of the book, which has a section on Hunters and Collectors.

Gudinski had founded Mushroom Records in Melbourne in 1972 when he was 20. As Stuart Coupe (2015: 5) writes in his biography of Gudinski:

> In Australia in the 1960s and 70s there was a large blues-based music scene and this is where Gudinski gravitated, particularly to the sounds of a Melbourne-based band called Chain formed in 1968. They were at the forefront of progressive blues in this country and Gudinski loved them. And he loved other, similar bands playing around Melbourne: Billy Thorpe and the Aztecs, early Chain lead singer Wendy Saddington, Carson, Madder Lake, and the Adderley Smith Blues Band.

Madder Lake signed with Mushroom and Gudinski released their first album *Stillpoint* in 1973.

Gudinski managed and booked some of the bands for the first Sunbury Pop Festival held on a farm outside of Sunbury about forty kilometres from Melbourne over the 1972 Australia Day long weekend. The festival attracted an audience of around 35,000. The bands included Billy Thorpe and the Aztecs, the Wild Cherries, Chain, Carson, who would all be described as Oz Rock, and prog rock bands including Tamam Shud and Healing Force. Describing the early period of Oz Rock, and showing his thorough dislike of that music, Walker (2005 [1981]: 7) writes: 'By the early '70s, a tradition was beginning to emerge in Australian rock, or "Oz-rock" – and what a repulsive one it was – Sunbury (another imported concept), Billy Thorpe, massively loud mindless boogie and gallons of beer.' Walker's point here about the Sunbury festival is that the idea originated in festivals overseas, most directly Woodstock. The Sunbury festivals became deeply associated with Oz Rock, not least because of the presence of Billy Thorpe and the Aztecs who played at all four Sunbury festivals. The very first Mushroom release was a triple album recorded at the 1973 Sunbury Festival.

Gudinski, along with Barry Earl, a music industry hustler, started Suicide Records in 1977 to sign punk bands. Earl had managed Mississippi who had a number ten hit in 1972 with 'Kings Of The World' and in 1975 transformed into the soft rock group Little River Band. Earl also claimed to have been instrumental in the La De Das moving to Australia from New Zealand where they had had five top ten hits. Punk was an area of music about which Gudinski knew nothing and Earl even less. The enterprise flopped after releasing a compilation album, *Lethal Weapons*, which included tracks by the Boys Next Door and also Teenage Radio Stars, a band which included Sean Kelly and James Freud both of whom were later members of the Models (see Coupe 2015: ch 8). In 1981 Gudinski started the sub-label White Records. Coupe (2015: 143) writes: 'This label had . . . resulted from brainstorming between Australian rock legend and then producer Lobby Loyde and Gudinski to launch a new label for what were deemed at the time to be "alternative" acts.' Loyde, a celebrated guitarist, had been in a number of rock bands including Billy Thorpe and the Aztecs and the Wild Cherries. Loyde was a better business partner for Gudinski than Earl had been. Coupe (2015: 140) writes that

> [Gudinski] sniffed something in Hunters. They were unique and arty, but Gudinski loved that – and their crowds were big. There was something there. So, comparatively early in their career, Hunters & Collectors were invited into the Mushroom offices for a meeting.

It is sometimes said that Gudinski set up White Records specifically for Hunters and Collectors. They were certainly the first band signed to the label and stayed on it for their entire recorded output. Although they were never a blues-rock band, the genre that Gudinski knew best, by the time of *Human Frailty*, Hunters and Collectors had shifted from being arty, and playing funk, being a part of the inner-city sound, to being a rock band in a style that Gudinski could appreciate.

Writing about Sydney, Graeme Turner (1992: 22) offers a more cultural take on the inner-city music scene:

> There was a point in the mid-1980s when there was a particularly sharp division between those alternative rock music fans who lived in the inner city suburbs in Sydney – Glebe, Paddington, Balmain, Darlinghurst – and those who lived in the west – Liverpool, Parramatta, Bankstown. . . . The inner city pubs were small and cliquey, while in the west the pubs were vast tunnels of noise littered with dead cans and plastic cups.

Turner suggests that the key moment for an inner-city sound in Sydney was the mid-1980s. In his 2005 Preface to *Inner City Sound*, for Walker, focusing on the artists, this period marked the end of the inner-city sound with which he was concerned. One reason for this divergence is that Walker was writing primarily about Melbourne while Turner's focus was Sydney.

While Walker was extolling the innovatory importance of the inner-city sound as against what he viewed as the boorishness and mundanity of Oz Rock, Turner took an opposing view. For him Oz Rock is simply Australian rock music and should be recognized as such:

> Australian rock music has always been firmly rooted in the suburbs and no matter how much it tried to adopt the cool cosmopolitan chic of a David Bowie or a Robert Palmer or an Annie Lennox, it always ends up sweating and screaming like Jimmy Barnes or Bon Scott or Chrissie Amphlett (Turner 1992: 22).

Shane Homan (2003: 170) takes a similar position to Turner:

> Despite histories to the contrary, Australian rock and roll had been a suburban experience from its origins in 1957. The suburban rock pub of the 1970s crystallised a complex relationship between audiences, performers and venues.

Bill Haley toured Australia in 1957, on a bill along with Gene Vincent and Little Richard, among others, spreading interest in rock 'n' roll and kick-starting Johnny O'Keefe's career from his previous cult following.[1] Lee Gordon, the promoter, had booked O'Keefe as the support act.

What has caused confusion is the use of the term pub rock to describe Australian rock music. As it happens, pub rock forms a pair with inner-city sound in that both describe places where music is played rather than generic characteristics of the music claimed to be played in those places. It is noteworthy that in the chapter on the pub in the book, *Myths of Oz*, published in 1987, co-written by John Fiske, Bob Hodge and Turner, four years earlier than Turner's chapter in *From Pop to Punk to Postmodernism* quoted from earlier, the section on rock music in pubs is headed 'Youth, Rock 'n' Roll and the Pub'. The term pub rock is only used in the label for a photograph of the Divinyls. However, over time pub rock has come to refer to the music made in pubs between the early 1970s and when the phenomenon petered out in the late 1980s and 1990s. What the term actually refers to is confusing. Is it all the music played in pubs or to a specific genre of music which happens to be that most commonly played by artists working in pubs? Perhaps the best example of the former usage can be found in the four CD collection called *The Glory Days of Aussie Pub Rock*, released in 2016. In the liner notes Stuart Laing (2016) writes:

> The truth of the matter is that pub rock in Australia in its 'glory days' was a surprisingly varied thing, something that was often (and often awkwardly) open to new influences, and something

_____

[1] It is worth listening to the CD *Rock'n'Roll Radio: Australia 1957* [Various Artists] which contains interviews with Bill Haley and other artists on the tour including Freddie Bell, Gene Vincent and Little Richard.

**Human Frailty**

that undoubtedly was a catalyst for the growth of our music and our culture.

Laing (2016) acknowledges that the music that dominated the pub scene was 'mostly blues-based' but includes all the other music being played in pubs including the music of the bands in the Carlton scene discussed in the Introduction.

The problem is that the powerful descriptive aspect of the term pub rock overlaps with the alternative term Oz Rock, used to identify a particular genre of music, and which actually may have its origin in Walker's construction in *Inner City Sound* of the music he disliked so much. In other liner notes to that same compilation, *The Glory Days of Aussie Pub Rock*, Anthony O'Grady (2016) makes a sociological argument for the development of the music others now call Oz Rock but which he calls pub rock. O'Grady distinguishes pub rock from the blues-rock played by Billy Thorpe and the Aztecs in the early 1970s in favour of the more straight-ahead, rock-based music which he identifies as beginning in,

> late 1976, coinciding with Dragon's breakthrough on radio with 'This Time'. By mid-'77 pubs – outer suburban beer barns to cramped inner-city taverns – were packed and boisterous. Pub rock took hold suburb by suburb, throughout capital cities and country regions.

O'Grady's argument is that pub rock was founded in an audience of young people, predominantly male (to which we can add white), a cohort in which unemployment in the late 1970s and 1980s reached double figures. For O'Grady (2016), 'pub rock was the sound of turmoil in suburbia'. He goes on:

'Blood and thunder blasted from The Angels' "Come Down", Cold Chisel's "Home And Broken Hearted", and Midnight Oil's "Don't Wanna Be The One".' O'Grady argues that the end of pub rock occurred in the late 1980s as a result of a combination of generational change and a structural economic shift in working-class occupations from the prevalence of blue-collar jobs to a more service-oriented economy. This latter development was discussed in Chapter 1.

Increasingly, terminologically Oz Rock is distinguished from pub rock. We have already seen Homan implicitly making this distinction. As he writes in a 2008 article: '"Oz rock" is most commonly used (in the mainstream Australian and overseas music media) to describe a local rock genre, which is then usually articulated to a national structure of practices' (Homan 2008: 601). In a 2014 article Paul Oldham (120) makes clear the relation between Oz Rock and pub rock: 'Oz rock was Australia's hegemonic style of pub rock from the early 1970s until the mid-1980s and arguably the first distinctly Australian popular music.' Oldham's point brings us back to the claim made by Turner, that Oz Rock should be understood as the mainstream rock music of Australia rather than just another popular music genre.[2]

In Victoria the so-called six o'clock swill only ended in 1966, whereas in New South Wales it had ended in 1954. Six o'clock closing had been introduced for pubs in New South Wales and Victoria, and also South Australia and Tasmania, in 1916 during the First World War. The consequence was that workers knocking off at 5:00 had to dash to the pub and drink as rapidly as possible.

---

[2] There were two main strands to Oz Rock, one developed in Melbourne and the other, slightly later, in Sydney (see Stratton forthcoming).

Opening later meant that pubs could offer entertainment. As Homan (2003: 226) writes about Sydney: 'The conversion of hotels into public entertainment centres was in some respects an unintended consequence of the amendments [in the 1954 Liquor Act] and constituted new regulatory problems.' In 1966 pubs in Victoria faced a similar situation. At this time in Melbourne groups played rock music in what were called discos, venues like the Thumpin' Tum and the infamous Catcher. These were essentially unlicensed coffee bars. Oldham (2014: 123) remarks: 'The constant resistance to the incorporation of venues serving liquor within the control of Melbourne's city planning made them an increasingly unattractive business venture and would contribute to the rise of pub rock.'

In an article from around 1968, Stephen Walker described Catcher:

> The most notorious club at the time was the Catcher in the dark, deserted & desolate end of Flinders Lane, an austere, painted black disused warehouse that you could hear from blocks away before you could even find it. It was a walk on the wild side, the surly sociopathic end of the rock music crowd slouched around a bare room listening to the harder and wilder end of the music scene. Bands like The Purple Hearts, Running Jumping Standing Still & The Wild Cherries raged until the early hours.
>
> There was a totally dark, mattress filled room called The Gobble Room and everyone had an edge that may have come from raiding their mother's diet pills. (Milesago undated (b))

The diet pills were benzedrine and other amphetamines which only became prescription drugs in the late 1960s. In

Brisbane, the band Lobby Loyde joined was called the Purple Hearts after the amphetamine used by mods in England. Two members of the band had migrated from London and one from Scotland. The Purple Hearts moved to Melbourne in early 1966. After that band broke up Loyde joined the Wild Cherries in 1967.

Perhaps the most important band that played Catcher, certainly for the evolution of Oz Rock, was Billy Thorpe and the Aztecs. Loyde, who had known Thorpe in Brisbane, joined the Aztecs in December 1968. By 1969 Thorpe had developed the loud, forceful blues-rock that became a characteristic of his music through the 1970s and of the evolution of Oz Rock in the pubs of Victoria. In 1970 Billy Thorpe and the Aztecs released the single, 'Rock Me Baby' with 'Good Morning Little Schoolgirl' on the B-side. The Aztecs' blues-rock built on the English blues-rock artists like the Groundhogs, Ten Years After and Savoy Brown who covered 'Rock Me Baby' on their 1968 album *Shake Down*. Nevertheless, The Aztecs' version is most similar to that by the American proto-hard rock group Blue Cheer. The Aztecs' version is faster and not as ponderous but works in the same heavy blues-rock territory.

This was the music the Aztecs were playing round Melbourne in the unlicensed clubs. Then, according to Thorpe, his agent Bill Joseph had a revelation:

> Bill called and said, 'Look, there's all these pubs out there that have got two men and a dog in them, one microphone, a two-foot stage and a single spotlight, and they hold 1200 people. Why don't we go out and look at hitting some of these pubs?' (Engleheart 2010: 20)

In this origin story, this is the moment when the popular blues-rock gets taken out of Melbourne's dry clubs like Catcher and into the licensed pubs where the music intersects with male audiences' consumption of large amounts of alcohol. In New South Wales and Victoria the drinking age had been eighteen since 1905 and 1906, respectively. In South Australia it was lowered from twenty-one to twenty in 1966 and to eighteen in 1971 and in Queensland the drinking age was lowered from twenty-one to eighteen in 1974 (see DrugFree.org.au 1998). Lowering the drinking age to eighteen, which had taken place in all states and territories by 1974, enabled the audience for rock music to enter pubs right across the country.

Going into the pubs was also the time when, with the help of their own PA systems, the Aztecs' music got even louder. Thorpe again:

> These rooms that we went into in the pubs were much bigger. Much, much bigger. So we took our own production in. The first couple of gigs, they were packed, but people just talked. You know, people got pissed and BLAH, BLAH, BLAH! Ranting. I said, 'Right, talk over this, you fucking cunts!' And that's how it all started. If you let an audience talk, they will, particularly where there's alcohol involved. (Engleheart 2010: 31–2)

For a different take on the beginnings of Oz Rock in pubs here is Rick Brewster of The Angels who, as we have seen, were from Adelaide but moved to Sydney:

> I was talking to someone who was running a venue in Melbourne at the time. He said to me he had never seen anything like it when *Face To Face* came out. He said as a

venue operator that was the beginning of pub rock: the style of music, the lyrics, the audience – and the venues were just packed to the rafters. The crowds were as loud as the bands almost. (O 2014)

*Face To Face* was The Angels' second album and was released in June 1978. Generically it did not have the blues-rock foundation that characterized Thorpe and The Aztecs' material. Regardless of the empirical truth of Thorpe's story, it brings together key elements in the shift of groups from playing the unlicensed discos to the licensed pubs.

Given Thorpe's story, we should pause here and think about the amplification for which Oz Rock bands in pubs were notorious. In one account:

[A] prominent feature that had manifested itself since Thorpe's move to Melbourne, and that by now had become synonymous with the Aztecs, was the volume. The band's manager, Michael Browning, coined a term that stuck: 'Aztec Energy'; describing the almost overwhelming power that the band generated from the stage. Billy had this to say about it to *Go-Set*'s [Molly] Meldrum in March, 1972: 'It was loud. Everything was loud. There was so much energy it was frightening in a way. I want to get much louder but the problem is that in this country the equipment can't handle it, and it just distorts so much of the sound. Hendrix was loud, but he was loud and clear'. (Milesago undated (a))

Playing in the Aztecs, Loyde used a 350-watt Strauss Warrior which, apparently, had to be regularly repaired (Hodgson 2010).

Many Oz Rock bands playing in pubs were similarly preoccupied with volume including Hunters and Collectors. In *Thirteen Tonne Theory* Seymour (2009: 269) writes that John Archer, the bass player, built a new bank of speakers:

> They were bass heavy and bass was what you needed most to cut through the walls of human flesh that were rapidly arriving at Hunters and Collectors shows. The Mixer [Robert Miles] had his ear. 'We have to overwhelm them' he said. . . . The PA had to cover a multitude of sins and crazed drunk people. They had to be controlled, their energy harnessed. For the next six years it worked.

This would have been some time after the *Human Frailty* album when Hunters and Collectors were firmly positioned as an Oz Rock band. We should note here again the rhetoric about volume being an energy. Seymour (2009: 270) adds: 'If being swept up by the blast of sound pressure was what they'd [the audience] come for, they got it.' Elsewhere, Seymour (2009: 277) has this insight about the relationship between alcohol consumption and the tremendous volume used by Hunters and Collectors:

> The band had become so loud on stage that it was effectively impossible to distinguish one instrument from another. I'll put it another way. Unless you were mildly drunk or deaf, it was unhearable. . . . Stage sound was a sonic assault that you drank to absorb.

As an Oz Rock band volume was an important aspect of Hunters and Collectors' music.

In his discussion of the aesthetics of rock music Bruce Baugh (2011: 8) tells us: 'Loudness, in good rock music, is also a vehicle of expression.' Loudness has also been of great importance in reggae sound systems. Here is Julian Henriques (2011: xv) describing the experience of extreme volume at the beginning of his book *Sonic Bodies*:

> It hits you, but you feel no pain – instead pleasure. This is the visceral experience of audition, immersed in auditory volumes, swimming in a sea of sound . . . There is no escape, not even thinking about it, just being there alive, in and as the excess of sound. Trouser legs flap to the bass line and internal organs resonate to the finely tuned frequencies, as the vibrations of the music excite every cell in your body. This is what I call *sonic dominance.*

Here again we have the idea of volume as part of the musical experience. Thorpe thought of volume as expressing energy. In Hunters and Collectors, Archer thought of the volume as a sonic blast overwhelming the audience.

At extreme volume sound waves immerse the body in the music to offer a totalizing experience. Steve Goodman (2012: 79) writes: 'Bass figures as exemplary because of all frequency bands within a sonic encounter, it most explicitly exceeds mere audition and activates the sonic conjunction with a modal perception: bass is not just heard, it is felt.' Bass is central to the experience of reggae. Archer was not only the bass player in Hunters and Collectors, he also built their early PA systems. Goodman (2012: 79) explains that, 'for many artists, musicians, dancers, and listeners, vibratory immersion [of the bass] provides the most conducive environment for movements of the body and movements of thought'. As Seymour writes, Archer understood the importance of bass as the foundation of the totalizing immersion of volume. We now have a way of understanding the importance of volume in the Oz Rock played in the pubs. Oz Rock may have been the sound of suburban turmoil as O'Grady suggests but the volume of the sound made it a site of complete audience involvement, a heightened experience transcending the mundane world of everyday life.

Oldham (2014: 129) identifies the key year for the development of Oz Rock: '1971 … marked a dramatic shift away from the dominance of the nightclubs towards the hotels, as well as civic centres and town halls as the central locations where live music was played and received.' Oldham (2014: 129-130) goes on to argue that the shift from the dry clubs to the licensed pubs also brought a change in the audience:

> Many of the texts describing this era (particularly rock biographies) highlight the aggressive and demanding nature of the working-class, suburban audiences that were increasingly outnumbering the scene's other key rock audience demographic: that of middle-class educated hippies who were followers of more sophisticated bands such as popular prog-rockers Spectrum, Mackenzie Theory, [and] art-rock mischief makers Captain Match Box Whoopee Band.

We can also read this as a move away from the inner-city scene that Walker thought of so highly to the suburban heartland of Australian rock that Turner and Homan identify. The legendarily large consumption of alcohol in a predominantly male environment suggests a cultural continuity with the six o'clock swill that, in Victoria, had only been abandoned a few years earlier. There was also a continuity with other aspects of Australian working-class masculinity, most obviously misogyny and violence. In a similar manner to that described by Oldham, as Hunters and Collectors shifted from an inner-city funk band to a suburban Oz Rock band their audience changed from mostly middle class to being more working class. Seymour (2009: 156) writes about how, 'To reach a pub audience, masculine power was what worked.'

Immersed in sound, often with the aid of beer, troubles and inhibitions disappear. The audience member lives in the moment outside of society but in an auditory world shared with other audience members. One way of thinking about this experience is in the terms of Mikhail Bakhtin's theorization of carnival. Peter Kohl (1993: 144), who has discussed rock music as a modern version of carnival, explains:

> The medieval European carnival consisted of a specific space and time in society in which all outside notions of space and time were forgotten. . . . Outside of carnival was a world of hierarchical structures: kings, noblemen, church officials held authority over the peasants and farmers of the land . . . But in carnival, according to Bakhtin, 'The laws, prohibitions, and restrictions that determine the structure and order of ordinary . . . life are suspended'.

Here I want to suggest that we can think of the Oz Rock pub gig as a version of carnival. To quote Kohl (1993: 143) again:

> The physical space of carnival is situated outside of everyday life and experience in our modern world. It's 'out there,' beyond the busy streets and neatly cropped hedges and well-lit store fronts. Its existence is quite literally on the edge.

Rather, we might say, carnival was in there, in the packed pub immersed in volume and alcohol, set apart from the trappings of suburbia.

This carnival can also be related to the Dionysian myth. In Paolo Euron's (2019: 10) description:

> According to the philosopher Friedrich Nietzsche, Greek tragedy has its origins in the Bacchus mysteries. . . . such celebrations were based on dance, music, excess, and wine . . . in order to create an ecstatic and orgiastic experience and the loss of the principle of individuation. In such an ecstatic, and orgiastic, experience, the individual forgets that it is a person and feels itself as a part of the whole of nature and life.

Bacchus was the Romanized Greek god Dionysius. As Euron (2019: 10) goes on to explain:

> According to Nietzsche, the Dionysian mysteries expose the tragic truth and are the original, tragic knowledge of life. What is the tragic truth? It is a non-rational truth. Existence is contradictory and without meaning, it is suffering and chaos. Rationality is a way to conceal this awareness, to cover the abyss and chaos of existence and to make life bearable.

We should be reminded here of Hunters and Collectors' early material, its preoccupation with social breakdown and the reference to Tadeusz Borowski's vision of a violent world of stone. We can think of the Oz Rock experience in the pub as a way of escaping the overdetermining, constraining rationality of modern, suburban life. Oz Rock offered the sonic experience of escape from the everyday life of unemployment and the imposed constraints of rational, middle-class society. We can think of this as a way to Dionysian ecstasy, through music, dancing and, in this case, beer rather than wine.

Fiske, Hodge and Turner (1987: 13) also liken the pub experience to Nietzsche's interpretation of the Dionysian ritual. They argue that, in this context: 'One meaning of drunkenness, then, is radical egalitarianism.' However, it was an egalitarianism only present in the carnivalesque time and space of the gig. Outside the gig, the forces of the state, most obviously, the police, reasserted control. It is often argued that the introduction of Random Breath Testing was one reason for the decline in audiences for the Oz Rock pub experience. RBT was introduced in Victoria in July 1976 and in New South Wales in December 1982. The state increasingly invaded the Dionysian, carnival space enforcing maximum crowd numbers, introducing noise limits and more rigorously policing the drinking age. Other factors included gentrification of the areas where the pubs that held Oz Rock gigs were, and changing laws about the presence of poker machines as well as the changes identified by O'Grady listed earlier. The Oz Rock gig entered a decline through the 1980s, particularly later in the decade.

The Australian rock tradition had been evolving in pubs, not only in New South Wales and Victoria but across Australia, since the early 1970s. By the time Hunters and Collectors made *Human Frailty* pubs were well-established venues and for Hunters and Collectors, as for other inner-city bands, there had developed a pathway from playing inner-city halls and small, local pubs to playing the large, suburban beer barns that had been pioneered by Billy Thorpe and the Aztecs in Melbourne and the first generation of Oz Rock bands in Sydney like AC/DC and Rose Tattoo.

However, we should not think that Oz Rock was only played in pubs. In 1974 AC/DC played many gigs in Chequers, a well-known Sydney nightclub, the Maroubra Surf Lifesaving Club, Ibrox Park High School in Leichhardt, Newcastle Town Hall, as well as the Hampton Court Hotel in Sydney and the Sandgroper Hotel in Leederville, Perth. In 1986 Hunters and Collectors played gigs at venues like Selina's in Sydney, the Newcastle Workers Club, Easts Leagues Club in Brisbane, universities including Macquarie, Deakin, Murdoch and the University of Queensland where I saw them, as well as various pubs across the country. As Hunters and Collectors moved from playing funk to playing rock, the shift to playing suburban pubs and clubs was inevitable and a move that had started before the band made *The Jaws of Life*, an album which, as we have seen, was steeped in the experience of travelling the isolated Australian roads between gigs. *Human Frailty* established Hunters and Collectors as one of the great Australian rock bands.

# **3**   Throw Your Arms Around Me

The most well-known track on *Human Frailty*, indeed one of Mark Seymour's most celebrated songs, is 'Throw Your Arms Around Me'. It has been released by Hunters and Collectors as a single three times, each time a different recording. Its first release was in November 1984, three months after the release of *The Jaws of Life* album. In some ways the single and the album could not be more different. The album charts an apocalyptic course across the vast Australian landscape. The single is a song of love and lust. However, the very dread with which *The Jaws of Life* is imbued is counterpointed by the desire, and indeed need, which founds 'Throw Your Arms Around Me'. When 'Throw Your Arms Around Me' was released the first time it failed to chart in Australia. In Aotearoa/New Zealand where the band always had a strong following the single reached number 28. In 1986 another version of 'Throw Your Arms Around Me' was recorded and placed as the second track on *Human Frailty*. Released as a single, in the wake of the success of the album, this time 'Throw Your Arms Around Me' reached number 49 on the Australian chart. Re-recorded and released again in 1990, the song climbed to its highest position of number 34. This version had been put on the *Collected Works* compilation released that year.

We should consider why Hunters and Collectors released three different studio versions of 'Throw Your Arms Around Me'. The first version was recorded on a digital two track at John and Paula's Hardware Street studio in Melbourne. It was produced by the band. Seymour has said the reason they re-recorded it was that 'the production wasn't good enough' (Sly 1986). The second version is the most well-known. It was produced by Gavin MacKillop who also produced the rest of *Human Frailty*. The first version is the most propulsive. It feels driven, less a ballad and more a cry of anguished love. The vocal sounds ripped out of Seymour. Compared to the first version the second is smoother, the highs in the guitar work have been toned down and Seymour's vocal is more under control. Seymour says that while making the album MacKillop 'convinced [him he] was a singer and we spent a lot of time on vocals' (Sly 1986). The overall arrangement is very similar to the first recorded version. However, the track is much more produced. Seymour explains:

> We double-tracked acoustic guitars, put acoustic harmonies on the electric guitar parts. We really went to town on this – real strings. At the end we just invented all these vocal harmonies in the studio, the whole band is singing there. (Sly 1986)

For some listeners the preference was for the starker first version but for most that version was unknown. The third version, from 1990, produced by Clive Martin who also produced the double platinum *Ghost Nation*, starts with what sound like processed clap sticks. It is slower and Seymour sings even more melodically and with less intensity than on the other studio versions. This version focuses more on Seymour playing an acoustic guitar. It

**Human Frailty**

62

sounds more like Seymour as a singer-songwriter. David Brearley, in an article in *The Australian*, remarks about the first version:

> It was Mark Seymour's first attempt at conventional melodic songwriting but the craft was all there. The performances were tough and sparse, and intimate, and the production was dripping with that stand-and-deliver authenticity that made Hunters the band they were. It was a beautiful song. (Brearley 2019)

However, Brierley (2019) goes on: 'Hunters took it back to the studio twice after 1984, loving it more tenderly for less effect at each pass.' That the band recorded the song three times suggests that they felt each time that the version they settled on did not do justice to the song.

'Throw Your Arms Around Me' has many unresolved tensions, the most obvious of which is the culturally 'feminine' quality of the lyrics, the vulnerability they show, while at the point in the band's career when they first recorded it, Hunters and Collectors were becoming a celebrated Oz Rock attraction. Each studio version attempts to resolve the tensions to make 'Throw Your Arms Around Me' a complete work. Each fails in a different way because the song exceeds the ability of any artist to contain the contradictions which generate the tensions. This, it would seem, is especially true when it is sung by males. The more 'masculine' the production, that is the more rock-oriented it is, the more at odds with this is the feminine quality of the lyrics. While Brearley prefers the first version, most commentators prefer the second.[1]

---

[1] The second version is the one recommended on the Hunters and Collectors' fan site, True Believers (undated (a)).

On this version, the band gives the song a harder beat and drives the ballad into more male, Oz Rock, territory (this gendering was discussed in Chapter 2), while the song remains a ballad. MacKillop brought a new and more objective perspective to the recording of the song. To make 'Throw Your Arms Around Me' work it is necessary to live with, and indeed work with, the contradictions that make the song so fascinating and special rather than trying to smooth them over or even erase them.

One thing that the increased chart position achieved by the song over its three releases signals is the increasing popular acceptance of the song as part of the Australian cultural imaginary. That the song wasn't just released three times but was recorded in studios three times, as well as being released on live albums in 1985, 1995 and 1998, tells us how central the band considered the song to be to their body of work.[2] After 'Throw Your Arms Around Me' was first recorded and released, its second release was as a live version on the album, *The Way To Go Out*, in 1985 which had been recorded at two gigs in August 1984 at the Earls Court ballroom, known as The Venue, in Melbourne's St Kilda. On that album 'Throw Your Arms Around Me' was situated as the first track as if somebody thought that, in spite of it being a ballad, it would attract people to the album. When the gigs were released as a video 'Throw Your Arms Around Me' was put third after 'The Way To Go Out' and 'The Slab'.

---

[2] The three live albums on which 'Throw Your Arms' Around Me appears are *The Way To Go Out* (1985), *Living in Large Rooms and Lounges* (1995) and *Under One Roof* (1998).

During the 1990s artists started covering 'Throw Your Arms Around Me'. In 1993 Vika and Linda Bull, along with Kate Ceberano, performed a version on the television show *Kate Ceberano and Friends* with, so Ceberano writes in her autobiography, a Hawai'ian island strum (Ceberano 2014: 154). The following year Ceberano, a soul and jazz singer, herself released a version on the album *Earth Music*, a collection of tracks by different artists made for the benefit of the Earth Music Trust to aid Australian land conservation and regeneration. This version is slowed down and has what sounds like an island strum counterpointed by percussion work by the highly regarded Ray Pereira. Ceberano appears to feel a special affinity with 'Throw Your Arms Around Me', duetting with Seymour on an acoustic version at the Mushroom 25 concert, a celebration of twenty-five years of the Mushroom record company, at the Melbourne Cricket Ground in November 1998. She re-recorded the song for her retrospective album of 1990s songs, *Nine Lime Avenue*, released in 2007. On this version Ceberano's smooth and contained, almost wistful, vocal is accompanied by piano and guitar.

Testifying to the song's increasing acceptance as an Australian standard, during the 2000s there have been covers by artists as diverse as Greg Page, better known as the Yellow Wiggle from the children's entertainment group; The Wiggles, who recorded the song for his album titled *Throw Your Arms Around Me* released in 2004; and by Tim Finn and Eddie Vedder for the album celebrating the career of Hunters and Collectors, *Crucible*, in 2013. According to the True Believers website devoted to all things Hunters and Collectors, up to 2014 Vedder, the lead singer of American rockers Pearl Jam, had performed the song thirty-three times as a solo artist and, with his group, twenty-one times.

Pioneered by the Bull sisters and Ceberano, the song has been increasingly covered by female artists. There is a live version by the Aotearoa/New Zealand artist Lorde on YouTube taken from a concert at the Sydney Opera House in 2017 where, sounding nervous, she sings with a piano accompaniment. When announcing the song she says she has never sung it before in public. Her nerves add a piquancy to the lyrics. In 2018 Missy Higgins included a live version on her greatest hits album, *The Special Ones*, and in the same year Alya performed a remarkable, slow and yearning version on the long-running TripleJ radio segment 'Like a Version'.

Sung by women, the song takes on a very different emotional tone than when sung by men. The male and female tension between voice and lyrics is resolved. To put it simply, it has been historically more accepted for women to ask for emotional support and love than for men. To sing the title phrase 'throw your arms around me' could be construed as a sign of weakness when voiced by an Australian male. Interestingly, in 2019 David Brearley argued that as the song has been more often covered so there has been a decrease in the emotional power expressed in the new versions. Referring to her second, more well-known, version, he wrote that Ceberano 'drowned [the song] in molasses' and went on to explain:

> This is the thing with Throw Your Arms Around Me. People invest it with too much gravitas. Successive versions get slower, more saccharine, more overwrought, probably more expensive, certainly more self-aware. (Brearley 2019)

The change Brearley identifies correlates with the increasing number of female covers of the song. These covers reconstruct the song in terms of female empowerment. There is the strength of asking, or even requesting, 'throw your arms around me' along with lines like, 'I will come for you at night time.' Female assertiveness became increasingly accepted as tenets of the feminist movement became embedded in everyday life from the 1990s onwards.

Brigid Delaney writes about 'Throw Your Arms Around Me' as a great Australian anthem:

> [T]he song comes on, and it barely takes a bar before we're all moving as one entity. You know what comes next . . . you've done it before on the best nights. You move closer and take the song literally. You're all howling the words, because you know them by heart, and you're armpit to shoulderbone, the song is a trigger for love, surges of it that feel so powerful and real. So many times in the pubs of my country town, I've screamed into the next ear 'I love you, man' while listening to this song, and meant it.

For Delaney it is a song that brings people together. It provokes love and community. However, we should not be misled by her vernacular use of 'man'. Delaney is describing a shared female experience. Men certainly sing Australian anthems in pubs, at barbecues, parties and similar events, but rarely this song of openness and love. They sing Cold Chisel's song about Vietnam War veterans 'Khe Sanh', or Chisel's song of lost love 'Flame Trees' or The Angels' 'Am I Ever Gonna See Your Face Again' which attracts the drunken, male audience response: 'No way, get fucked, fuck off' (see Tait 2010: 171).

We should remember that on *Human Frailty* 'Throw Your Arms Around Me' is the second track on the album, coming after 'Say Goodbye'. It appears strange to have a song so lyrically preoccupied with desire coming immediately after a track about the end of a relationship where it is the woman who is finishing it. However, much of *The Jaws of Life*, the previous album, was concerned with the road. Indeed, the final track on that album, 'Little Chalkie', includes the lines 'And my town, it is a teacher / All trucks and beers and memories spread out on the road.' Written in the first person, 'Say Goodbye' starts with the protagonist coming home 'After three months of constant grind and travel.' We don't know what he does, he could be a touring muso like the members of Hunters and Collectors or he could be a truckie, but he has returned from the boundless, apocalyptic Australian land outside the coastal cities. For Chris Johnson (2008), 'His love, or his ability to at least express it, had been stolen. The vast distances out there had put miles between him and the closest beating heart.' 'Say Goodbye' marks a transition to the more personal and intimate songs of *Human Frailty*. Nevertheless, it is a song of rejection. The singer goes round to his girlfriend's house where 'She ground her finger into my breastbone / And she said, she said / "You don't make me feel like a woman any more."' The repetition of 'she said' builds tension released in the shouted statement by the girlfriend, voiced by Seymour, repeated verbatim in a downward cadence.

In performance the audience, mostly male, often drunk, would join in yelling this phrase along with Seymour. Here we have the antithesis of the audience response to The Angels' question, Am I ever gonna see your face again? The Hunters and Collectors' audience, with Seymour, took on the character of the girlfriend assertively telling her boyfriend that he has failed in his masculinity to make her feel like a woman. We don't know if this is sexually or in acknowledging her emotional needs as a woman, or both. Describing this phrase, Johnson (2008) calls it a 'gender-bending but somehow unifying creed'. In itself, the phrase can be read as a commentary on the breakdown in communication between men and women in Australia. Chanted by a predominantly male audience it comes from a complex place of homosociality where men find support in other men, and especially as their relationships with women break down. In Australia this is a version of what is commonly identified as mateship. Nick Dyrenfurth (2015: 17) defines mateship as 'the bonds of loyalty and equality, and feelings of solidarity and fraternity, that Australians, usually men, are typically alleged to exhibit'. The shouted phrase in 'Say Goodbye' at once unifies the male audience in a common experience of female rejection while situating them as feminised, something that happens but is often unsaid, in the homosocial practice of mateship. Seymour (2009: 156) writes in *Thirteen Tonne Theory*: 'The Singer's frailty and confusion. Energies clashed – the band's machismo and the Singer's weakness.' Seymour seems often to have felt feminised against what he perceived as the traditional male attitudes of his bandmates.

Sarah French (2017: 46) has described a vignette by the neo-burlesque dancer Finucane called 'Consumption has done for her'. Here, Finucane lies in bed apparently incapacitated by tuberculosis performing the stylized expressions associated with this 'woman's illness'. She then throws the doona aside to reveal her body in a tasseled silver bikini. Accompanying this is 'Say Goodbye' which, as French (2017: 46) writes, is 'sung in a male guttural voice, which is immediately at odds with the image of a bikini-clad woman'. French (2017: 46) comments that the vignette 'demonstrate[s] a subversive feminist intent'. The impact of the male voicing of the line here is to call into question the patriarchal cultural association of assertive women with being in some way masculine. What links 'Say Goodbye' with 'Throw Your Arms Around Me' is the problematization of characteristically Australian male-gendered behaviour.

Seymour has often told the story behind 'Throw Your Arms Around Me'. The most detailed version is in *Thirteen Tonne Theory* (Seymour 2009). It seems Seymour's mother met a young woman of Chinese heritage in a library and after chatting with her thought she and her son might get on so she gave the young woman, May was her name, Seymour's phone number. She rang him. Already we have a gender reversal: the girl making the first move and ringing the boy, rather than the other way round. What might have given Seymour's mother the idea that the two had things in common? The most likely explanation is that May had been brought up in country Victoria where her parents had a farm. Seymour's family was from Benalla, a town of under ten thousand people, also in country Victoria, about two hundred kilometres northeast of Melbourne. They moved to Melbourne in 1972 when Seymour would have been about sixteen so he was very much a country boy. It was a very intense relationship; at least we know it was for Seymour. He has described it as the first time he fell in love. 'Throw Your Arms Around Me' emerged out of Seymour's feelings for May.

When he has talked about the relationship Seymour has mentioned that May had a copy of Van Morrison's album *Astral Weeks*. Seymour had known the album for a few years. When the band were in London in 1983 he shared a bedsit with Geoff Crosby who at that time played keyboards with Hunters and Collectors: 'I'd perform cook-ups on the two-burner stove … while listening to *Astral Weeks* on the Synth Player's cassette machine' (Seymour 2009: 104). *Astral Weeks* had been released in 1968. The critic William Ruhlman (undated) writes: '*Astral Weeks* is generally considered one of the best albums in pop music history, but for all that renown, it is anything but an archetypal rock & roll album.' Morrison was backed by a group of jazz session musicians. Ruhlmann (undated) explains:

> The freewheeling, loose feel adds to the intimacy and immediacy in the songs. They are, for the most part, extended, incantatory, loosely narrative, and poetic ruminations on his Belfast upbringing: its characters, shops, streets, alleys, and sidewalks, all framed by the innocence and passage of that era.

Given Ceberano's liking for jazz, it may be this subterranean jazz influence in 'Throw Your Arms Around Me' that is one reason for her continuing interest in the song.

*Astral Weeks* is not in any ordinary sense an album of love songs. Rather, as Bruce Springsteen has noted, it gave him 'a sense of the divine' (Michaud 2018). Perhaps for this reason, given the intensity, the feeling of its transcendental quality, of his love, Seymour seems to have associated *Astral Weeks* with his relationship with May. Talking about the composition of 'Throw Your Arms Around Me', Seymour has said:

I remember when I came up with it I was listening to Van Morrison a lot, and I'd come out of the Crystal Ballroom kind of punk scene and that idea of something being sung with that level of sensitivity and with such delicacy with a romantic feeling – it was just all new territory for me. (Justice 2016)

As a solo artist, starting in 1997, he has played live the closest *Astral Weeks* has to a love song, 'The Way Young Lovers Do' (see True Believers undated (b)). While 'Throw Your Arms Around Me' is a very different kind of a song to anything on *Astral Weeks*, including 'The Way Young Lovers Do', the album provided a model for the new kind of intimate ballad that Seymour wanted to write.

'Throw Your Arms Around Me' is a song that, lyrically, mixes, as I have already remarked, love and lust. It is impossible to find where one ends and the other starts. Underlying it is the unease of Catholic guilt. Seymour has described growing up in an overwhelming Catholic environment where his grandmother, his father's mother, would monitor all speech and actions for religious transgression. At the evening meal as a child he would sometimes unknowingly say something that distressed her:

There'd be gloomy walks the next day. Little chats down the end of the garden. Mum's soulful murmurings into her husband's ear, to help him get back on his pony while his mother went into the full bedroom retreat, intoning endless rosaries to assuage even the slightest possibility that she might not make it to heaven now, having borne witness to some dreadful comment a child had made in complete innocence. (Seymour undated)

Seymour (undated) goes on to tell us: 'Anything to do with God, sex, or defecation somehow rattled the cage.' Years later this proscriptive Catholic influence can be found in many of Seymour's lyrics. For example, in 'The Slab' on *The Jaws of Life*, with lyrics commonly considered to be about cunnilingus, we have: 'Out here in the street, naked in front of God and everyone / I'm beginning to see daylight yawning down there.' One can only imagine the sheer horror Seymour's grandmother would have felt at the mention of cunnilingus if, that is, she even knew of what that sexual activity consisted. At the same time, Catholicism holds the belief that God sees everything. As Kenneth Baker (1982: 138) explains in his *Fundamentals of Catholicism*: 'Since God sees everything from all eternity, his plan is established in that light.' The tension generated by Seymour's, possibly unacknowledged, guilty anxiety helps drive the power of the track. 'Throw Your Arms Around Me' derives much of its potency from the guilt in the lyrics' secular expression of desire.

There is a cover of the track by the comedy group The Doug Anthony Allstars who had reformed for a charity performance in 2003. Paul McDermott, also brought up a Catholic and known for the purity of his singing voice, inserts Lord into the lyrics: 'I will raise you from your sleep / Lord, I will kiss you in four places.' The song immediately takes on a religious quality. Being raised from sleep now is reminiscent of Jesus raising the dead Lazarus back to life. In her description of the song, Delaney (2014), who was also brought up a Catholic, writes: 'There is nothing that comes closer to Australia's secular hymn (but also an enticing booty call) than this song.' We should be reminded of the conversion of African-American gospel songs into soul songs. How, for example, a lot of the emotional power of Ben E King's 'Stand By Me' (1961) comes from its spiritual roots in gospel. King, who co-wrote the song, recalled that the title derives from the gospel song 'Stand By Me, Father'. Of course, 'Throw Your Arms Around Me' has no gospel origin but Seymour's expression of secular desire is deeply influenced by his Catholic background.

Here we can retell a story about May. Towards the end of their relationship, she took Seymour out one night to the nearby park, enjoined him to stay still and silent and then fed possums who came and sat round her. When Seymour (2009: 162) recounts this story in *Thirteen Tonne Theory* he writes that May reminded him of St Francis of Assisi 'only Chinese and female' feeding the animals. For May, feeding possums was likely something she had done on the farm where she grew up. She wanted to share a special experience with her lover, not be compared to a Catholic saint.

As Delaney remarks, 'Throw Your Arms Around Me' is played at major events in life, weddings and even funerals. Yourgoingtohear meroar (2019) writes in the Comments section of the song on YouTube:

> Love this song! Played it at my husband's funeral in 2010. He died 5 days before his 41st Birthday. Never forgotten. Genuine Aussie bloke with a big heart and soul xo.

The kiss and hug at the end of the comment are the key here. Now the imperative to throw your arms around me is from the loved one left behind to the one who has passed over.

The song carries an underlying feeling of the closeness of death. In part this comes from Seymour's Catholic childhood again. He writes:

> My grandmother believed in 'hell'. It was so real to her that if a child blasphemed at the dinner table there was every possibility we were all doomed simply for having heard the word at the wrong time. (Seymour undated)

With such a belief death is an ever-present fear. It dictates life. Delaney (2014) understands this:

> Maybe 'Throw Your Arms Around Me' is played at life's milestones because this song takes us to the edge of life – and of course at this edge is where energy and life force and the realisation of the whole shebang's frivolity burns and flares together. You dance on the edge.

In Chapter 1 I discussed Richard Lowenstein's remarkable video for Hunters and Collectors' first single, 'Talking To A Stranger'. It visualizes a post-apocalyptic landscape. In this interpretation of the song, as Seymour (2009: 66) renders it: 'The "stranger" was some mythical beast of the future that roamed the horizon on the edge of the sea, or lurked deep inside the dreamscape of the song'. This mythical beast is a materialization of the existential dread, the fear of death and the possibility of hell, which Delaney detects at the edge of life in 'Throw Your Arms Around Me'.

In the lyrics 'throw your arms around me' is not a request. It's a plea for contact. It's not, I'll throw my arms around you. It is asking, begging, that you throw your arms around me. comfort me; take away my existential fear, my anomie. In one of his books on the philosopher Søren Kierkegaard, Christopher B Barnett (2011: 207), quoting the theologian Thomas Merton, writes:

> [The Christian mystic] confronts a kind of 'existential dread', understood as a 'sense of insecurity, of "lostness", of exile, of sin', but faces it in 'direct dependence on an invisible and inscrutable God, in pure faith'.

In a similar move to that made in soul songs, 'Throw Your Arms Around Me' substitutes the loved one for God. On occasion this becomes apparent in the lyrics. Why does the lover kiss the beloved in four places? Other singers have found this obscure. Neil Finn of Crowded House, on a whim, changes the number of kisses each time he sings the song. A common view is that the four relate to erogenous zones on the loved one's body. Johnson (2008) argues that the song goes 'way beyond mere blood and love into a kind of religious lust, a born-again desire to kiss her in those unnamed "four places" – the four points of the cross'. In Catholicism the kiss has a sacred quality. We should remember the kiss that Judas gave Jesus. The priest kisses the altar. He also kisses the cross. In 2018 Cardinal Sean O'Malley spoke to the soon-to-be priests of Boston and identified, coincidentally, four kisses:

> There are four kisses of the Catholic priest. The priest kisses the altar. The priest kisses the Gospel. The priest gives a kiss of peace to his people. The priest kisses the cross. (O'Malley 2018)

Making the connection between the secular and the religious, there is also the kiss between bride and groom in the wedding ceremony. The singer's kisses transcend the secular, transcend desire, and take on a spiritual connotation.

Johnson (2008) goes on to equate the four kisses with the four points of the compass, making the loved one, perhaps, an uncanny land like Australia to be explored. We might think here of John Donne's poem 'To His Mistress Going to Bed', written some time around the turn of the seventeenth century, which Seymour may have studied during his Arts degree. There we find Donne, with a religious overtone, appreciating his mistress' nakedness by relating her in a proto-colonial turn of phrase to the discovery of the New World: 'Oh my America! my new found land, . . . How blest am I in this discovering thee!' In Seymour's lyrics Australia takes the place of America and Seymour's beloved, May, replaces Donne's mistress.

In the lyrics to 'Throw Your Arms Around Me', Seymour tells us: 'I met you in high places / I touched your head and touched your feet.' Dating from around the twelfth century BCE, there was an association of high places with religious worship, a practice the Israelites inherited from the conquered Canaanites. The Temple Mount in Jerusalem is the most sacred of these high places. Meeting his loved one in a high place connects her to the sacred but also to the land, something reinforced by the idea of touching her head and her feet. In Taoism the Chinese ideograms for Tao includes the characters for head and foot. It suggests the life force, qi, which flows through the chakras in the body. In traditional Chinese thought, when you are standing on the ground with bare feet, energy from the earth enters your body (Williams 2018). More generally this is known as grounding or earthing. In Seymour's lyrics, the Australian land, uncanny for settler Australians, includes diverse spiritual high places – Seymour uses the plural, high places – those of the settlers but importantly including the sacred sites of the Aboriginal people. As Gelder and Jacobs (1998: 1) note about the settler Australian experience, 'far from being out of place in Australia, [Aboriginal sacredness] sometimes seems . . . to be *all over the place*' [italics in original]. In the lyrics of 'Throw Your Arms Around Me', high places are multiple if not everywhere. It is in these high places that the singer has met his beloved.

In 'Throw Your Arms Around Me' the loved one, by virtue of being loved, is mystical and sacred, and connected to the uncanny land which, we have seen in Chapter 1, was the earlier preoccupation of Seymour and Hunters and Collectors. This concern with the land would not go away and would return to the forefront on the album *Ghost Nation* where, again, the land of Australia would be represented as uncanny, haunted, if not, as it was for its first inhabitants, sacred. Here, though, in 'Throw Your Arms Around Me', it is the beloved who is invested with these qualities and desire for her is expressed as the resolution, albeit ultimately an impossible resolution, of the contradictions that lie at the basis of the song.

# **4** The other tracks

*Human Frailty* is a strange name for an Oz Rock album. It doesn't have the aggressive quality of Rose Tattoo's *Assault and Battery* (1981) or The Angels' *Night Attack* (1981), or the suggestion of seediness that can be found in Cold Chisel's *Breakfast at Sweethearts* (1979) where Sweethearts was a cafe in Kings Cross, the entertainment and red-light inner-city suburb of Sydney. Further, the term was not new for Hunters and Collectors. The band had been using it since 1982. In *Thirteen Tonne Theory*, Seymour (2009: 49) provides this account of the term's origin:

> The Doctor [Doug Falconer, the drummer, who has a medical degree] went off with the Manager [Michael Roberts] the following week and began the process of negotiating a publishing contract with Mushroom Publishing. He came back with a document. It was passed around. 'We are now a registered company called "Human Frailty Pty.", and the contract is drawn up between it and the publisher. We are all directors of the company so we all have to sign it.'[1]

In this narrative Seymour's primary concern is not with the use of Human Frailty but the realization that copyright in the

---

[1] In other versions of the band's history Roberts became their manager later, about the time of the release of the *The Way To Go Out* live album in May 1985.

songs will be shared equally by all members of the band. This is an irritation which haunts *Thirteen Tonne Theory*. Mushroom Publishing was an arm of Mushroom Records. Having signed to Mushroom Records in 1981, the next step was a music publishing arrangement. Human Frailty Pty. incorporated the band as a company to sign with Mushroom Publishing. Jack Johnson (1986) notes that the first appearance of the new Hunters and Collectors company was on the single 'Run Run Run' in 1982. In Australia this was included, as a separate 7" single, with the band's first album. This suggests that whatever the origin of the term for the band, it had been in use for at least four years before the band decided to use it as the title of an album.

Seymour himself sees *Human Frailty* as a milestone in the career of Hunters and Collectors. In Chapter 3 we saw that Seymour was very clear after *The Jaws of Life* that he wanted to write pop songs. Was 'Throw Your Arms Around Me', possibly the song for which the band is most well known, a pop song in Seymour's way of thinking? Perhaps, but 'Throw Your Arms Around Me' had been first recorded, and released as a single, back in 1984. We can note that it carried the Human Frailty company acknowledgement. It seems that there was a concern among some members of the band about including the track on the new album because it suggested a weaker, less masculine image, than the one they wanted to portray. Perhaps, though, this was Seymour's point. Pop in Australia has historically been associated with the feminine, in practice female artists, from Little Pattie to Kylie Minogue, and female audiences. Rock has been thought of as a masculine genre.

One aspect of *Human Frailty*'s feminine quality is that its songs are about relationships and about love in particular, not about conquest and sex. In *Thirteen Tonne Theory*, Seymour (2009: 156) comments:

> *Human Frailty* changed everything. The exotic wilderness was a thing of the past. It was about love now. . . . These were pop songs. It was 1986 and Hunters and Collectors wanted success. Three years later radio came across.

Success in the terms Seymour is using means popular recognition, record sales and, as a consequence, the band earning more money. Although Hunters and Collectors continued generically as an Oz Rock band, Seymour is signalling a change in the audience he was addressing, an opening up to a new female audience. We have already seen this in the discussion of 'Throw Your Arms Around Me'. While not directly looking for a female audience, his songs shift from a macho celebration of the road, to starting to question some of the underlying assumptions of the male Oz Rock audience. *Human Frailty* established contradictions between the songs' lyrics and the audience's homosocial assumptions.

What, then, does Human Frailty mean? Frailty suggests weakness, a lack of strength whether that be physical, mental or moral. It has been suggested that Robert Miles came up with the term, 'in response to the group's attempt to find a word or phrase to describe fear' (RockPortraits 2014). This begs a number of questions. First, why were the band looking for a term to describe fear? Second, why name the band's joint company after a term they use for fear? And third, why then use the term for what they hoped would be the band's breakthrough album? Fear that can be understood as the human experience of existential dread permeates *Human Frailty*. In Chapter 2 I have already remarked on this as the driving force through Hunters and Collectors' early work. It is what stands behind the relationships described in the album's songs. From this point of view, having two break-up songs bracketing the album, 'Say Goodbye' and 'This Morning', suggests the dread from which we are protected by relationships. It is love and other emotions related to love, or at least relationships, that keep us from experiencing dread. Fear is inherent in relationships and surfaces as a relationship ends. In *Human Frailty* it is the relationship that keeps fear at bay. The fear of the loss of the relationship is not only the fear of losing the loved one but is also the fear that the ultimate fear, dread, will no longer be kept at bay. Here, for Seymour, and Hunters and Collectors, it is relationships that spare us from dread. The monster that is existential fear, dread, patrols outside the relationship waiting to pounce if the relationship weakens or ends.

There is a more prosaic understanding of the novelty of *Human Frailty* in Hunters and Collectors' oeuvre. In an interview at the time of the release of the album, Seymour explained, 'they're [lyrics] all domestic because politics begins and ends in the home' (Sly 1986). Here, it is suggested that we should think of the album as political. The connection Seymour is drawing here is with the second wave feminist idea that the personal is political. Carol Hanisch popularized this slogan when it was used as the title for an essay she published in 1969 – though Hanisch has disputed that she came up with the phrase. In a 1981 academic article, Linda Nicholson discussed the background to the term:

> This focus [on the home by the women's movement] developed out of a growing awareness of the obstacles a woman's 'special role' within the home raised to her full participation in the public sphere and because of an awareness of the disparities between her situation within the private sphere and the ideals of the public sphere. From this focus on the home and on interpersonal interactions emerged the slogan 'The personal is political'. (Nicholson 1981: 96)

Here we should remember Seymour's Arts degree. Taking his degree around 1980 he would have been well aware of second wave feminism and its history in Betty Friedan's 1963 book, *The Feminine Mystique*. Friedan's book was founded in a critique of the conventional role of woman as wife and mother centred in the domestic sphere of the home.

The politics of the domestic is central to 'The 99th Home Position', a track on *Human Frailty* rarely discussed yet which provides a fundamental insight into the concerns of the album. This track is one of the album's most straightforward rockers. Its beat is described in a review (Double 2020) as a 'stonking shuffle'. It's a track made for dancing. The simplicity of the rhythm disguises the complexity of the lyrics which critically, though possibly ambivalently, engage with traditional gender roles that place the woman in the home and the man working outside. The lyrics begin: 'If the man must be / Sleepin' at home all the time / And the woman must be / Out workin' all the time'. The sentence isn't completed. Instead the lyrics offer a commentary on what those who follow the dominant ideology would regard as a disturbing disruption of traditional gender roles and suggests that, in the end, 'They all gotta go / Back to home position'. The ideological claim is that the social order is founded on these gender roles. Mayhem would follow if they break down. The continuation of the social order requires a return to the 'home position'. The force of the lyrics critiques this but read literally they could be understood as endorsing this gender conservatism.

Thinking of *Human Frailty* in terms of the politics of the domestic environment helps to make sense of the two tracks which are not about relationships: 'Relief', the fifth track, and 'Is There Anybody In There', the eighth. 'Relief' is an anti-war song from the point of view of a mother. It is about a mother's despair at the injuries suffered by her soldier son. The song might have fitted better on the following album, *What's a Few Men?* This album is more overtly political. Its title, and the track of the same name on the album, derives from a story about the Australian troops at Gallipoli in Albert Facey's memoir *A Fortunate Life*:

> Some time later we had a distinguished visitor – a high ranking British officer. He came along our main frontline trench with several of our staff officers and commanding officers. He got a whiff of the smell coming from No Man's Land and asked the Australian officers, 'Why don't you bury the bodies?' Our Commanding Officer explained that the Turks opened fire every time this was attempted and we had lost men trying. The officer's reply to this shocked all of us who heard him. He said 'What are a few men?' We referred to him as 'Lord Kitchener' from then on. (1981: 264)

'Relief' is in the tradition of Australian anti-war songs from the 1970s and the 1980s. These include Eric Bogle's 'And The Band Played Waltzing Matilda', released in 1971, Cold Chisel's 'Khe

Sanh', released in 1978 and Redgum's 'I Was Only 19', released in 1983. The Australian Vietnam moratorium campaign against the Vietnam War ran through 1970 and 1971. Australian combat troops were withdrawn by late 1971. The war finally ended in 1975. In Australia the trauma of the war lasted well after the return of the young men, many themselves traumatized, who had been conscripted to fight. These songs express that ongoing trauma. In 'Relief' the mother sleeps, bringing her relief, and the soldiers sleep in death. They are 'gorgeous bodies / Primed and ready in the sun'. Commenting on 'Relief', Seymour suggested, in an interview when *Human Frailty* was released, that the track was 'probably one of the strongest songs on the record'. Judging from the apparent lack of times it was played live this opinion was not shared by the rest of the band. Or perhaps 'Relief' was just not suitable as an Oz Rock track. It fits better with Seymour's later, post-Hunters and Collectors solo work.

'Is There Anybody In There' is a critique of the experience of television in the home. Although the lyrics refer to Ronald Reagan, their description of watching bleeding, bandaged and dead soldiers is more relevant to the way that the Vietnam War was directly broadcast on television into people's lounge rooms. In the refrain, Seymour sings 'Don't leave it uncovered / Better cover it over'. He is referring to the television set itself. In his commentary on the track in the liner notes for the 'best of' collection called *Natural Selection*, Seymour (2003) launched a vitriolic attack on television: 'Television is evil. Like alcohol and penicillin, it can be beneficial if taken in moderation, but is always lethal in large doses'. Like 'Relief', 'Is There Anybody In There' can be considered an anti-war song. As Jessie Kratz (2018) writes about the Vietnam War: 'Since it was visible in their homes [on television], Americans were able to connect and empathize with the soldiers more than ever before'. The same point could be made about the Australian television audience. 'Is There Anybody In There' is lyrically a track which suggests that television transforms war into spectacle.

The track on *Human Frailty* that most clearly shows the album's shift from the band's earlier material concerned with the road and the open space of the Australian landscape to the domestic environment is 'The Finger'. Lesley Sly (1986) describes the track as: 'An odd song. Very claustrophobic'. Seymour responds:

> That's good, because that's what it's about. This and 'Throw Your Arms' are the oldest songs on the record. Here I was trying to describe coming in from the landscape to a tiny little room. (Sly 1986)

This sense of the size and openness of the Australian land is what David McComb with the Triffids conveyed in 'Wide Open Road', also released in 1986. Like 'Say Goodbye', discussed in Chapter 3, and 'This Morning', 'Wide Open Road' is a break-up song: 'The sky was big and empty / My chest filled to explode / I yelled my insides out at the sun / At the wide open road'. The road is a male domain. It is a place that destroys relationships. In his essay for the Hunters and Collectors' boxset *Horn of Plenty*, Chris Johnson (2008) describes the truckies who drive the road trains across the enormous distances:

Cry for your mother, cry for your father, and drive on. Sing your tough songs as clouds gather blue. Speed toward the pinpoint horizon.

In 'Say Goodbye', the singer has come home 'After three months of constant grind and travel' only to be accused by his girlfriend of not making her feel like a woman any more. Far from being unconditionally supportive, the domestic domain is where girlfriends and wives make the Australian male feel he has not lived up to expectations.

Home is an enclosed space, the opposite of the openness of the land over which have been built the roads that connect the dispersed Australian cities and towns. However, in these songs home is not a place of easeful relaxation. It is claustrophobic. In 'The Finger', Seymour is referring to the home he shared with May, the girlfriend who inspired 'Throw Your Arms Around Me'. In the liner notes for *Natural Selection*, he explains that it was:

A bedsit the size of a small caravan, over the top of a bistro in Fitzroy Street. It was cheap, with a view. There was a large bay window next to the bed that received the full blast of a prevailing south westerly, and at night we lay there, listening to the rain pounding on the tin roof, or the drug dealers and junkies scuffling in the alley below. (Seymour 2003)

What makes this claustrophobic bedsit bearable, what makes this domestic domain home, is the presence of his lover: 'We made the whole building sway / Made the whole city shudder / You off in one corner / And me back here in the other'. The lyrics oppose the description of the grime of the room with the love, implied in desire, of the couple within it. In good times this is what Seymour, and other men like the truckies, come home to from the vast, uncanny land.

Lyrically, 'Dog' can also be read as a song about a relationship. Literally, it describes a dog's relationship with its mistress, named Hazel in the lyrics, from the dog's point of view. Central to 'Dog' is the idea of submission: 'It's all comin' out into the open and I'm licking your hand all over.' What is coming out is the love the dog feels for its mistress. Love here seems to be associated with abasement, and the suggestion is that the dog has tried to hide its feelings. If the lyrics are read as a displacement of a human relationship, it is clearly unequal. What makes it unequal is love: 'Here is love and the world well lost.' Love weakens the dog, for which we should read the man, who becomes submissive because of his love for the woman who is his mistress. This positioning of this woman echoes that in 'Say Goodbye' where the man goes round to see his girlfriend and is rejected. In these lyrics strong women make men feel inferior and spurned. Love, for men, is a weakness. We are returned to the album's title, human frailty.

In this world where the domestic domain is experienced as confining, love affairs inevitably end badly. Rebecca Hawkings has discussed masculinity in Australian rock music of the 1970s and 1980s in terms of what she calls hyper-heteromasculinity. She developed the term following the work of Daniel Mosher and Mark Sirkin on what they call hyper-masculinity which they define,

> as a particular type of aggressive macho personality, consisting of three components: (a) callous sexual attitudes towards

women, (b) violence as manly, and (c) danger as exciting. (Hawkings 2014: 2)

Adding in the emphasis on heterosexuality, Hawkings (2014: 2) argues: 'This script of masculinity . . . shapes the construction of Australian rock music of the 1970s.' To which we can add the 1980s. She goes on: 'Australian rock music, particularly in the 1970s and 1980s, was a space within which the "script" of a hyper-heteromasculine national identity was reiterated and reconstructed' (Hawkings 2014: 3). It is no wonder that the relationships sung about in *Human Frailty* end badly.

In *Thirteen Tonne Theory*, Seymour (2009: 155) writes: 'I wrote a song about [my room] with her in it. "The Finger". I wrote about the room with her not in it, "This Morning".' The album ends with 'This Morning', a song of anguish and yearning, about the experience of a relationship break-up. In the *Sonics* interview, Seymour describes the track as: 'Epic. The big one' (Sly 1986) and goes on to suggest that the song exemplifies the 'new Hunters' as compared, it is implied, with the Hunters of the road in *The Jaws of Life*. 'This Morning' is a big, dramatic ballad. In its emotional power it might be compared with 'Throw Your Arms Around Me'. That song, as we have seen, is about love and desire. 'This Morning' conjures the emotions at the end of a relationship. If 'The Finger' tells us that what makes the tiny bedsit where the singer felt confined if not trapped, bearable is the loving relationship, 'This Morning' is founded on the emotional experience of loss. Where, in his commentary on 'The Finger' quoted above, Seymour felt cosy sharing the bed with his lover while the rain poured down outside, in 'This

Morning', evoking the pathetic fallacy, 'Storm water's weeping on my bedroom window'.

At the core of 'This Morning' is the terrible need that the lover will change her mind, that she will stay after all: 'But blind faith's / Trying to tell me it isn't over.' In its theme, 'This Morning' is reminiscent of the Beatles' song 'For No One' on their 1966 album *Revolver*. There, Paul McCartney sings: 'You want her, you need her / And yet you don't believe her / When she says her love is dead / You think she needs you.' There is a French horn in the bridge of 'For No One' and a French horn interweaves through the melody of 'This Morning'. Discussing the use of the French horn in Hollywood film music, Erika Wilsen (2021: 8) comments: 'The horn is not only a conveyor of heroism and noble purpose, but also evokes yearning, love, sadness, loss, pain, and nostalgia.' It is the latter qualities that the French horn is most commonly used to summon up in popular music. For example, the French horn is used in Neil Young's 1970 track 'After The Gold Rush' where the overarching feeling is of loss and nostalgia. In 'This Morning', as in 'For No One', the mournful lower notes of the French horn suggest the sadness and regret the singer feels at the end of his relationship. In both cases, 'This Morning' and 'For No One', it should be pointed out, it is the woman who is leaving.

If in *Human Frailty* we should think, as Seymour advises us, about the personal as being political, then we should also acknowledge that the tracks are dominated by break-ups, anxiety and jealousy. There is 'Everything's On Fire', a song about temptation and jealousy: 'And if I don't come home before midnight / And I call out your name in the dark / You'll know that I've been tempted / And I'll know that I've got no heart.' For the author of *Rock Portraits* (2014), the lyrics equate sexual desire with flames. We could think here of Madonna's 'Burning Up', released in 1983, in which the female singer is on fire, 'burning up for your love'. In one reading of 'Everything's On Fire', the lyrics are about love and desire, about how inconceivable it is that the male singer won't come home and has, therefore, been successfully tempted to go off with another woman. In this event, desire turns to fiery destruction of his relationship but, metaphorically, of the home, the house, the confining domestic domain. Seymour (2003) himself offers another reading which positions the lover as being unfaithful: 'A hymn to love going wrong . . . very quickly. The guy is outside with a jerry can full of hero, and murder in his heart . . . not a how to'. Hero is a brand of engine oil that might be used as an accelerant. In this reading, the cuckolded boyfriend is literally going to burn down his lover's house. We should remember here Hawkings' discussion of Australian males and their propensity for violence, often against women. For Seymour, the lyrics are about domestic violence.

The lyrics of the fifth verse connect fire with masturbation: 'So to all of you feelers and fumblers / Waiting for the fireworks to start / [in a whisper] Do it yourself.' The lyrics then make a further connection with violence: 'Unbutton the butcher in your heart.' Unbuttoning here suggests opening the trouser flies and the butcher suggests the penis as both sexually and violently aggressive. Butchers chop up dead meat. The reference to heart signals the emotional drive of sexual arousal. We are offered a dense image which brings together sex, fire and violent male power in the context of a song about lust and jealousy. Released as a single the track climbed to number 78 on the Australian chart. The video for the track includes shots of buildings on fire. According to Seymour (*Natural Selection* liner notes), Molly Meldrum refused to play it on the ABC television music show *Countdown*. Perhaps this was because of the video's implied violent content or perhaps because Meldrum thought it might encourage pyromaniacs; probably both. The lyrics carry an echo of Talking Heads' 'Burning Down The House', released in 1982, where they sing: 'Some things, sure can sweep me off my feet / Burning down the house.' We shall meet Talking Heads again shortly.

Musically, *Human Frailty* stands at the intersection of Hunters and Collectors' move from being a funk-related band to being a rock group in the Australian Oz Rock tradition. As *Human Frailty* consolidated that move it also signalled the greater input of Seymour as a lyricist. For the band the move was thought of as a shift from the white funk influence of Talking Heads to the rock tradition of the Rolling Stones. Discussing *The Jaws of Life*, Seymour remarked on the band members' liking for the Stones:

> Instead of looking at what was happening around us we decided we'd play music that reflected what we used to be like and what we've always been like. And we looked at incredibly un-chic bands like the Stones. We used to really like the Stones – we'd always leap around suburban lounge rooms listening to the Stones. So we started playing rhythms that had that feel. (Brown 1985)

That feel was the blues-influenced rock that permeates the music of the Rolling Stones. However, Hunters and Collectors played with a bass, drums and guitar set up which had evolved playing funk.

In 2014, when a reformed Hunters and Collectors supported the Rolling Stones for a gig at Mt Smart Stadium in Auckland, Seymour told an interviewer that his special memory of the Rolling Stones was: 'Listening to "Brown Sugar" on my sister's turntable in my bedroom, through headphones, while studying integral calculus and ignoring my father, 1974.' The Stones' influence, which clearly went back well into Seymour's teenage years, is more pronounced on *Human Frailty* than on *The Jaws of Life*. As Seymour has remarked about the driving rock sound of 'Everything's On Fire': 'It came about with me, John and Doug playing a Stones sort of feel. We wanted to write a soul sort of song' (Sly 1986).

In his book on funk, Rickey Vincent (1996: 36) writes:

Good funk music (and much of jazz) is designed to allow the listener to focus on any instrument and hear a complete musical statement, yet the instrument still remains viable within the group. While rock artists were content to drive power trios, funk bands were consistently large.

This was certainly true of Hunters and Collectors who had started out as an ensemble unit of thirteen players. Among these, as was typical in funk groups, the bass, played by Archer, was important not because it complemented the drums creating a strong rhythm section but because it functioned as a melodic instrument in its own right, counterpointing the rhythm played by the drums and harmonizing with the melody played on the guitar. By the time of *Human Frailty* it was clear that the band functioned with a core trio of bass, drums and guitar/vocal; Archer, Falconer and Seymour.

In the way the bass functioned in Hunters and Collectors there remained a significant difference between Archer and the Stones' Bill Wyman. Discussing Hunters and Collectors, the author of *Rock Portraits* (2014) explains:

> In many bands bass is virtually an invisible instrument; it's important, but hard to notice. That's not the case here. Archer's bass lines feel like they weigh tons, yet snap and bounce like rubber. This is the legacy of the band's interest in funk, a bass-heavy sort of dance music.

In comparison, Ryan Madora (2014) comments on the Stones' bassist:

> Playing with a distinctively 'rooted' mindset, Wyman clearly defines the harmony of the song, which happens to be just the right thing for rock and roll. He inherently knows just the right place to jump up an octave, creating a sense of motion even though the harmony remains the same.

Archer has always been a funk bass player where Wyman, working with Charlie Watts, the Stones' drummer, was a rock player. Archer's bass playing functions similarly to a lead guitar. It is up front and dynamically intersects with Falconer's drums and Seymour's vocals and guitar. It remains a funk bass while the band, slimmed down, functioned more and more like a rock band.

Talking Heads had moved in the other direction, from playing rock to playing funk. David Byrne has commented:

'We wanted to develop an understanding of the African musical concept of the interlocking, interdependent parts and rhythms that combine to make a coherent whole' (Henke 1980). As we have seen, the white funk of Talking Heads was influential on the Melbourne alternative scene in the post-punk, late 1970s including on early Hunters and Collectors. White funk, sometimes described as angular funk, is the funk structure that is heavy on the bass and counter rhythm, but without the swing of the funk of, for example, James Brown or Parliament. Vincent (1996: 34–5) argues that swing is an important aspect of funk. He describes 'the tendency to generate a swing' in funk and argues: 'The funk music of the late sixties generated a groove so wicked it should be called a "swang"'. Rock has no swing. Talking Heads had funk but no swing.

What made the Stones exceptional in the rock world was Watts' ability to swing. Watts had started out as a jazz drummer and his idols were all jazz drummers such as Art Blakey and Elvin Jones. As Tony Sokol (2021) puts it: 'His jazz training put a swing feel to strict patterns. He made regular rock-and-roll beats dance and bounce.' Most rock drummers keep a straight beat. In an interview with Russell Brown for *Rip It Up* in 1985 Seymour says:

> I think there's this thing called the Great Aussie Tug, which Doug [Falconer] always talks about, that some bands have. It's a kind of an R&B laziness, because you've got a real straight square beat, but it's got this walking tempo – it's very traditional in a lot of ways, but the way Australian bands play R&B, they always have that taut but lurching a little bit feel. AC/

DC are a classic example, Rose Tattoo, X, the Birthday Party had it. (Brown 1985)

Seymour recounts how after their return from England in late 1983 but before Perano left the band and when Hunters and Collectors were still thought of as a white funk band, X supported them one night at the Manly Tavern. Hunters and Collectors were blown away: 'They were a three-piece rock band that played a kind of deep, grinding R&R, with a singer who howled in agony and a bass player who slammed the beat into the floor' (Seymour 2009: 123). X was Ian Rilen's band in which he played bass and subsequently guitar. It was formed before Sardine v and reformed after it which is when Hunters and Collectors played with them. Rilen had been in Rose Tattoo, one of the early Oz Rock bands, before X. X were a kind of alternative, much harder, post-punk Oz Rock band. Seymour wanted Hunters and Collectors to sound similar.

In Australian rock, to follow Seymour's paraphrasing of Falconer's point, the drum may be a little behind the beat but it is still square to it. Consequently the rhythm feels jarring rather than easily moving from beat to beat. The description of R&B laziness refers to the lack of swing. This is what separates AC/DC from the Stones. We should remember the importance of swing in Charlie Watts' playing. This has been key to the sound of the Stones and an important component in what made the Rolling Stones so distinctive as a rock band. Hunters and Collectors were like the Australian bands listed by Seymour. They never swung, even as a funk band, but they had a driving beat.

On *Human Frailty*, the rock influence is most obvious in the band's cover of 'Stuck On You', a track written by Rilen and his then wife Stephanie Rilen. 'Stuck On You' had been first recorded by the Rilen's group Sardine v. This is another song about a failing relationship. Sung by Stephanie, the singer has heard that her partner has been 'out and getting round' while she is 'stuck here and stuck on you'. The Sardine v version uses a Farfisa organ. The Hunters and Collectors' version begins with a rather dirty viola playing the melody. Played live, Hunters and Collectors substituted Jack Howard on his trumpet. Seymour's vocal enters before the drums and bass, moving the distress in the lyrics more to the front in the mix. The anguished frustration of the singer is reinforced by the French horn which weaves through the verses. In this rock song the drums and bass work together to present a driving beat similar to, but slower, than the rock sound of 'Everything's On Fire'. Together with Seymour's masculine, harsh vocalization the effect is to generate a more aggressive impact than on the original where the reedy sound of the Farfisa organ complementing Stephanie Rilen's thinner vocal sound and a slower, more stately drum beat, gives the track a more plaintive tone.

*Human Frailty* is an album of productive contradictions. It is a rock album in the Oz Rock tradition but it continues to have funk elements, especially in the way the bass functions. *Human Frailty* is identified as an Oz Rock album but its concerns are centred on love and loss rather than the usual preoccupations of Oz Rock which were founded in sex and violence. It is a political album but with a politics based in the personal not in any economic or institutional political sense, so unlike the politics in the songs of Midnight Oil. *Human Frailty* is an album about relationships yet it is mostly about failing relationships, about emotions like lust and jealousy. It is an album much of which is danceable but an album where an audience can sing along and find meaning in the lyrics. What makes *Human Frailty* successful is that these contradictions, a magnified version of those in 'Throw Your Arms Around Me', work together dynamically to produce an album which audiences found both complex and energizing.

# **5**  After *Human Frailty*

After *Human Frailty*, Hunters and Collectors went on to be one of the mainstays of the pub rock circuit until the band retired in 1998. During those twelve years the band released another five studio albums and two live albums, one of which, *Under One Roof*, was recorded near the end of their farewell tour at Selina's in the Coogee Bay Hotel in Sydney. Four of the studio albums charted in the top ten in Australia and the fifth, *What's a Few Men?*, the album released after *Human Frailty* in 1987, got to number 16. Live albums were popular releases for Oz Rock bands. Most released at least one during their career, Australian Crawl released two and Cold Chisel released four. Oz Rock bands often felt that studio recordings failed to capture the energy and intensity of their performances which, as we have seen, included a potent immersion of the audience in the music. This was certainly the case with Hunters and Collectors who released three live albums in total during their career. Both the ones after *Human Frailty* made the top fifty in Australia and both were certified gold.

Even more than *The Jaws of Life*, *Human Frailty* was an album where Hunters and Collectors were transitioning into a rock band. After *What's a Few Men?*, the band took on a guitarist. Barry Palmer joined in 1988 and first played on *Ghost Nation*, released in 1989, continuing with Hunters and Collectors until the end. Palmer had joined the Melbourne rock band Harem Scarem before their second and final album, *Pilgrim's Progress*, released in 1986. He was a lead guitarist with a blues-rock background. With his inclusion Hunters and Collectors became sonically much more a guitar-based rock band. Derived from the band's funk history, Archer's bass playing had had a lead quality, laying down a groove which often worked contrapuntally with Falconer's drumming. In the tracks on *What's a Few Men?* through to *Ghost Nation* the bass increasingly played as part of the rhythm section with Falconer and Seymour, giving the band a more traditional rock sound.

By the final albums, the focus is on Seymour's lyrics. The production puts Seymour's vocals up front in the mix. His voice has become the centrepiece of the band. At the same time, Seymour's vocal tone has modulated and smoothed out so that rather than the half-shouted, half-sung vocals, with rasp, which often sound like they are wrenched out of his body, that were characteristic of Seymour's work on the albums up to and including *Human Frailty*, the vocals become much more focused in his voice with an emphasis on the lyrics. Increasingly a key site of the band's connection with its Oz Rock audience was lost while the band attracted a more diverse audience.

On the back of the release of *Ghost Nation*, the local edition of *Rolling Stone* named Hunters and Collectors their Band of the Year in 1990 and the album was nominated for Album of the Year in the ARIA awards. The first single from the album, 'When The River Runs Dry', which reached number 23 on the chart, the highest placing of any Hunters and Collectors single until 'Holy Grail' in 1993, was nominated for Best Single and the accompanying video for Best Video. If *Human Frailty*

Human Frailty

was Hunters and Collectors' breakthrough album to the Oz Rock audience, *Ghost Nation* broke the band into a more mainstream audience. This included their singles getting played on rock radio stations. In the previous chapter I quoted Seymour in *Thirteen Tonne Theory* commenting that three years after *Human Frailty*, radio started playing the band's recordings. Seymour is referring to *Ghost Nation*, with its rockier sound and smoother vocals. In this context it is not surprising that *Ghost Nation* and the two following albums, *Cut* and *Demon Flower*, all made the top ten of the album chart.

*Ghost Nation* returns to some of the themes Seymour raised in the albums before *Human Frailty* but in a more direct and measured way. Jack Howard (2020: 106) describes Hunters and Collectors as socially conscious and compares the band to Midnight Oil: 'Mark's lyrics were more psychological, more urban and socio-political than The Oils' up-front issue-related political songs.' The track 'Ghost Nation', for which the album was named, is a commentary on the settler Australian experience. It expresses Seymour's ambivalence about the country: 'Too old to move, too rich to ignore / Garden of Eden on the South Pacific shore' but also 'Empty playground, drenched in sorrow'. This is a line which can be read as again referencing the genocide of the Aborigines. Australia is identified as a paradise built on the extermination of the country's Indigenous population. It is, of course, not a Garden of Eden. This is the illusion of terra nullius. The colonizers destroyed what might be thought of as a Garden of Eden. The final line, 'Ghost nation's soul can never be sold' begs the question of whether the ghost nation is that of the murdered Aborigines or the settler Australians. Their presence appears so certain but is always already called into question by the ghosts of those killed to make way for the uncanny Australian nation. The lyrics of 'When The River Runs Dry' also reference the destruction of Indigenous society linking it with the settler disregard of the imperatives of the natural world or, as the lyrics put it: 'Turn your back on Mother Nature'.

As *Human Frailty* included a cover of 'Stuck On You', *Ghost Nation* includes a version of 'Crime Of Passion'. Covering this track, like covering 'Stuck On You', is a recognition and acknowledgement of Hunters and Collectors' origins in the 1970s Melbourne alternative scene. 'Crime Of Passion' was written by Eric Gradman and Elizabeth Reed, a well-known Melbourne photographer who has photographed many local rock musicians (see Murray 2011). Gradman had played in the Bleeding Hearts, sometimes described as an early Oz Rock band. Gradman: Man & Machine released 'Crime Of Passion' as a single in 1979.

The lyrics of 'Crime Of Passion' are founded in obsession and murder. They begin: 'Is that love in your eyes? Or just obsession?' and culminate with the male singer murdering his lover: 'Can anybody hear if I cry out loud? In confusion / I had the bloody knife – I did what I did this time / There's blood on the floor, there's blood on the walls / There's blood on my hands'. In 'Crime Of Passion' the man murders his lover in what he thinks of as self-defence because of what he believes to be her all-consuming and destructive obsession. In its concerns, 'Crime Of Passion' lifts off from Talking Heads' 'Psycho Killer', released in 1977 on that band's first album. We have already noted the importance of Talking Heads to Melbourne's late 1970s alternative scene.

'Crime Of Passion' can be read as playing out the French section of 'Psycho Killer': 'Ce que j'ai fait, ce soir-là – What I did, that evening / Ce qu'elle a dit, ce soir-là – What she said, that evening / Réalisant mon espoir – Making real my hope (rendered better in English as dreams) / Je me lance vers la gloire – I throw (launch is less literal but would be a better translation) myself towards glory'. If we can assume this is about murder, it is about a man, identified as the singer, killing a woman. In key ways, 'Crime Of Passion' plays out this idea and this structure. The most important difference is that in 'Crime Of Passion' the man imagines the woman is obsessed with him and he murders her to protect himself from her. 'Crime Of Passion' offers a motive for the murder where 'Psycho Killer' implies the killer simply wants to kill. He is, after all, a psychopath. The Australian revision suggests a failed relationship. In this way the track is of a piece with many of the tracks on *Human Frailty*. 'Crime Of Passion' is based on Australian males' violence towards women, discussed in Chapter 4. The lyrics can be understood in terms of extreme domestic violence. In Australia around 1990 on average significantly more than one woman a week was murdered by her current or former partner (see Carcach and James 1998). It is possibly not a coincidence that both 'Crime Of Passion' and the 'Stuck On You' were co-written by women. Both suggest the obsession that underlies much domestic violence.

Like 'Stuck On You', 'Crime Of Passion' is one of Hunters and Collectors' best rockers. This is partly because the lyrics are so direct – there is a clear narrative – and also because they are more buried in the mix than the lyrics of most of Hunters and Collectors' tracks. The Gradman version has a pronounced martial beat. There is also a strong emphasis on Gradman's voice. Rather like some of Lou Reed's vocals with the Velvet Underground, the lyrics are almost recited as if performance poetry. The Hunters and Collectors' version is much harder and much more a rock song. *Ghost Nation* was produced by the Englishman Clive Martin, who had worked as the engineer on albums by Queen and Nick Cave and other rockers and, suggesting a further Talking Heads connection, had worked with David Byrne. In Australia in 1988 Martin post-produced the pub rock band Painters and Dockers' album *Kiss My Art*. Signalling their connection with Hunters and Collectors, Howard had played on their first album, *Love Planet*, released in 1985. Hunters and Collectors' version of 'Crime Of Passion' has a strong Rolling Stones influence evidenced in the way the rhythm section was mixed. In a key departure from the Gradman original, the Hunters and Collectors version includes a riff played by Palmer reminiscent of one used in the Stones track 'Honky Tonk Women', released in 1969, where it was played by Keith Richards. Rising out of the mix and coupled with the fecund energy of Seymour's vocal, the riff gives the Hunters and Collectors version a driving force transforming 'Crime Of Passion' into a hard rock classic.

The album after *Ghost Nation*, *Cut*, released in 1992 and climbing to number 6 on the album chart, contains the track that competes with 'Throw Your Arms Around Me' for its sedimentation into Australian culture. However, 'Holy Grail' is not a love song, it is a song about desire for something that is out of reach. Seymour has said he had been reading a Jeanette Winterson novel, *The Passion*, published in 1987, and 'Holy Grail' is based on ideas suggested by that novel about Napoleon's doomed march into Russia in 1812. The legend of the Holy Grail has a long mythical history which in one account has it as the chalice, perhaps given to Joseph of Arimathea, which held Jesus' blood after he was crucified. The quest for the Grail is a key motif in legends associated with King Arthur.

The idea of the quest is central to the success of Seymour's song. Seymour has explained that he was thinking of his search for success for Hunters and Collectors in America. His own quest is described in the second verse: 'Started out / Seeking fortune and glory / It's a short song but it's a / Hell of a story,.' . . . 'I'm still a fool for the Holy Grail'. However, it is through sport that the song has embedded itself in Australian culture. 'Holy Grail' is another anthem. It seems that after the release of *Cut*, the Queensland Bulls cricket team, playing in the national Sheffield Shield competition, started singing the song in their dressing room to increase their motivation. The team had never won the Shield. When they did finally succeed in the 1994/1995 season, Hunters and Collectors were asked to sing 'Holy Grail' on the Bulls' home ground in Brisbane, the Gabba.

Later in the decade, 'Holy Grail' became associated with Australian Rules football. In *Thirteen Tonne Theory*, Seymour (2009: 352–66) tells a story, with some important inaccuracies (see KJ 2011), about how in 1994 the band were invited to play as the pre-game entertainment at the final of the national preseason Australian Rules competition. Seymour went on to perform solo at the 1998 Australian Football League (AFL) Grand Final after Hunters and Collectors had broken up and also the 2009 Grand Final when he performed on a bill with Jimmy Barnes and John Farnham. In 2013 the reformed Hunters and Collectors performed at the AFL Grand Final as the halftime entertainment. 'Holy Grail' was on the set list every time. Reinforcing the link between 'Holy Grail' and AFL football, after Channel Ten won the television rights in 2002 it used the song for four years during its Saturday live and Grand Final broadcasts (see Gill 2013).

In the years since they broke up Hunters and Collectors have become increasingly acknowledged as one of the great Australian bands. Since the millennium they have reformed a number of times playing benefits and one-off concerts, and short tours. As we have seen, 'Throw Your Arms Around Me' has become an Australian standard. 'Holy Grail', now inextricably linked with sport in Australia, has also become an Australian anthem. Hunters and Collectors' tracks are now a fixture of Australian rock radio alongside those by AC/DC, Cold Chisel, Midnight Oil and INXS.

The reputation of *Human Frailty* continues to increase. In 2008 an episode of SBS (Special Broadcasting Service) television's *Great Australian Albums* was devoted to *Human Frailty*. In 2010 John O'Donnell, Toby Cresswell and Craig Mathieson (74), three well-known Australian music critics, placed *Human Frailty* at number 18 in their book on *The 100 Best Australian Albums*. *Human Frailty* is not just a great Australian album; it has become a respected part of Australian popular culture.

# References

Anon. (2014), 'Rolling Stones: Bedlam bliss at the town hall', *New Zealand Herald*, 22 November. Available online: https://www.nzherald.co.nz/entertainment/rolling-stones-bedlam-bliss-at-the-town-hall/RHR54ZBANXWTFHAFOTKDIV35JQ/?c_id=1501119&objectid=11362451 (accessed 16 June 2022).

Baker, K. (1982), *Fundamentals of Catholicism, Volume 1: Creed, Commandments*, San Francisco: Ignatius Press.

Barnett, C. B. (2011), *Kierkegaard, Pietism and Holiness*, New York: Routledge.

Baugh, B. (2011), 'Prolegomena to Any Aesthetics of Rock Music', in M. Spicer (ed.), *Rock Music*, 3–9, Surrey: Ashgate.

Bongiorno, F. (2015), *The Eighties: The Decade That Transformed Australia*, Victoria: Black Inc. Books.

Borowski, T. (2021), 'The World of Stone: A Narrative in Twenty Pictures', in M. G. Levine (trans.), *Here in Our Auschwitz and Other Stories*, 223–80, New Haven, CT: Yale University Press.

Bourke, C. (1997), *Crowded House: Something So Strong*, Sydney: Macmillan Australia.

Brearley, D. (2019), 'Hunters and Collectors: When an Anthem Goes Astray', *True Believers: Hunters and Collectors*, 20 July. Available online: https://humanfrailty.com.au/?page_id=10167 (accessed 13 June 2022).

Brown, R. (1982), 'Seek and vs Shall Find', *Rip It Up*, 1 November. Available online: https://paperspast.natlib.govt.nz/periodicals/RIU19821101.2.49 (accessed 10 June 2022).

Carcach, C. and M. James (1998), 'Homicide Between Intimate Partners in Australia', *Australian Institute of Criminology*:

*Trends and Issues in Crime and Criminal Justice*, July. Available online: https://www.researchgate.net/profile/Carlos-Carcach /publication/237539998_Homicide_between_Intimate _Partners_in/links/5845a56c08ae2d2175681a5a/Homicide -between-Intimate-Partners-in.pdf (accessed 14 June 2022).

Cassel, B. (undated (a)), 'Big Night Music Review by Bill Cassel', *AllMusic*. Available online: https://www.allmusic.com/album/ big-night-music-mw0000195703 (accessed 25 May 2022).

Cassel, B. (undated (b)), 'Hunters and Collectors Review by Bill Cassel', *AllMusic*. Available online: https://www.allmusic.com/ album/hunters-collectors-mw0000854013 (accessed 25 May 2022).

Ceberano, K. (2014), *I'm Talking: My Life, My Words, My Music*, Sydney: Hachette Australia.

Clifforth, J. (2020), 'I Was In-Between Two Worlds', in D. Nicholls and S. Perillo (eds), *Urban Australia and Post-Punk: Exploring Dogs in Space*, 27–33, London: Palgrave Macmillan.

Coupe, S. (2015), *Gudinski: The Godfather of Australian Rock 'N' Roll*, Sydney: Hachette Australia.

Crnković, G. (2000), *Imagined Dialogues: Eastern European Literature in Conversation*, Evanston, IL: Northwestern University Press.

Dark Entries Records. (undated), 'impLOG – Holland Tunnel Dive', *Dark Entries Records*. Available online: https:// darkentriesrecords.bandcamp.com/album/implog-holland -tunnel-dive (accessed 9 June 2022).

Delaney, B. (2014), 'Australian Anthems: Throw Your Arms Around Me—Hunters and Collectors', *The Guardian*, 25 February. Available online: https://www.theguardian.com /music/australia-culture-blog/2014/feb/25/hunters-and -collectors-throw-your-arms-around-me (accessed 13 June 2022).

Delaney, M. (1982), 'Talking to a Stranger: Extensive Early Interview with Geoff Crosby and Greg Perano', *True Believers: Hunters and Collectors*, 25 September. Available online: https://humanfrailty .com.au/?page_id=3562 (accessed 25 May 2022).

Donne, J. (c1593–6), 'To His Mistress Going to Bed'. Available online: https://www.poetryfoundation.org/poems/50340/to -his-mistress-going-to-bed (accessed 17 June 2022).

Double J. (2020), 'Hunters & Collectors – *Human Frailty*', *ABC*, 17 February. Available online: https://www.abc.net.au/doublej /programs/classic-albums/hunters-and-collectors-human -frailty/11966870 (accessed 13 June 2022).

Drugfree.org.au (1998), 'Under Age Drinking: Develop Policy Options to Reverse the Present Trend Facing Australia', Available online: https://www.drugfree.org.au/images/pdf -files/library/alcohol/UnderAgeDrinking.pdf (accessed 13 June 2022).

Dyrenfurth, N. (2015), *Mateship: A Very Australian History*, Brunswick, VT: Scribe Publications.

Engleheart, M. (2010), *Blood, Sweat and Beers: Oz Rock from the Aztecs to Rose Tattoo*, Sydney: HarperCollins Australia.

Euron, P. (2019), *Aesthetics, Theory and Interpretation of the Literary Work*, Leiden: Brill.

Facey, A. (1981), *A Fortunate Life*, Fremantle: Fremantle Press.

Fiske, J., B. Hodge, and G. Turner (1987), *Myths of Oz: Reading Australian Popular Culture*, North Sydney: Allen & Unwin.

French, S. (2017), *Staging Queer Feminisms: Sexuality and Gender in Australian Performance, 2005–2015*, London: Springer Nature.

Gelder, K. and J. Jacobs (1998), *Uncanny Australia: Sacredness and Identity in a Postcolonial Nation*, Melbourne: Melbourne University Press.

Germana, M. and A. Mousoutzanis (2014), 'Introduction: After the End?', in M. Germana and A. Mousoutzanis (eds), *Apocalyptic*

Discourse in Contemporary Culture: Post-Millenial Perspectives on the End of the World, 1–14, New York: Routledge.

Gibson, S. (1994), 'This Rock is Sacred': The Northern Territory Government and the Handback of Uluru (Ayers Rock-Mount Olga) National Park, November 1983–May 1986, Grad Dip. Arts (History), Northern Territory University. Available online: https://ris.cdu.edu.au/ws/portalfiles/portal/35837165/Thesis_CDU_34583_Gibson_S.pdf (accessed 10 June 2022).

Gill, S. (2013), 'Is 'Holy Grail' Our AFL Grand Final Anthem?', The Roar, 13 September. Available online: https://www.theroar.com.au/2013/09/14/is-holy-grail-our-afl-grand-final-anthem/ (accessed 14 June 2022).

Goodman, S. (2012), Sonic Warfare: Sound, Affect, and the Ecology of Fear, Cambridge, MA: MIT Press.

Hawkings, R. (2014), '"Sheilas and Pooftas": hyper-heteromasculinity in 1970s Australian popular music cultures', Limina: a journal of historical and cultural studies, 20 (2): 1–14.

Henke, A. (1980), 'Talking Heads add some funk', Rolling Stone, 16 October. Available online: https://www.talking-heads.nl/index.php/talking-heads-archive/135-talking-heads-add-some-funk (accessed 14 June 2022).

Henriques, J. (2011), Sonic Bodies: Reggae Sound Systems, Performance Techniques, and Ways of Knowing, London: Bloomsbury Publishing.

Hodgson, P. (2010), 'Tone Down Under: A Brief History of Vintage Australian Tube Amps', Premier Guitar, 13 September. Available online: https://www.premierguitar.com/gear/tone-down-under-a-brief-history-of-vintage-australian-tube-amps (accessed 13 June 2022).

Homan, S. (2003), The Mayor's A Square: Live Music and Law and Order in Sydney, Newtown: Local Consumption Publications.

Homan, S. (2008). 'An "Orwellian Vision": Oz Rock Scenes and Regulation', *Continuum*, 22 (5): 601–11.

Howard, J. (2020), *Small Moments of Glory: The Man Behind the Mighty Hunters & Collectors Horn Section*, Cammeray, NSW: Simon & Schuster.

Johinke, R. (2009), 'Not Quite *Mad Max*: Brian Trenchard- Smith's *Dead End Drive-In*', *Studies in Australasian Cinema*, 3 (3): 309–20.

Johnson, C. (2008), 'Horn of Plenty Essay', *True Believers: Hunters and Collectors*. Available online: https://humanfrailty.com.au/?page_id=555 (accessed 10 June 2022).

Johnson, J. (1986), *Human Frailty* review, *The Ward Report*, 4 September. Available online: https://humanfrailty.com.au/?page_id=3808 (accessed 15 June 2022).

Justice (2016), 'Interview: Mark Seymour Talks Twilight Shows!', *Spotlight Report*, 5 February. Available online: https://spotlightreport.net/music/interview-mark-seymour-talks -twilight-shows (accessed 13 June 2022).

Kennedy, D. (2012), 'Eddie Mabo, the Man Who Changed Australia', *BBC News*, 6 June. Available online: https://www.bbc.com/news/magazine-18291022 (accessed 9 June 2022).

KJ. (2011), 'Dear Mark Seymour . . .', *Our Big Expat Adventure*, 11 April. Available online: https://ourbigexpatadventure.wordpress.com/2011/04/11/dear-mark-seymour/ (accessed 14 June 2022).

Kohl, P. (1993), 'Looking Through a Glass Onion: Rock and Roll as a Modern Manifestation of Carnival', *Journal of Popular Culture*, 27 (1): 143–62.

Korff, J. (2021), 'Aboriginal Land Rights', *Creative Spirits*. Available online: https://www.creativespirits.info/aboriginalculture/land /aboriginal-land-rights (accessed 9 June 2022).

Koulermos, G. (1983), 'Hunters and Collectors', *Cashbox*, 10 December.

Kratz, J. (2018), 'Vietnam: the first television war', *Pieces of History: National Archives*. Available online: https://prologue.blogs. archives.gov/2018/01/25/vietnam-the-first-television-war/ (accessed 16 June 2022).

Laing, D. and J. Brown (2014), 'Liner Notes', *(When the Sun Sets Over) Carlton (Melbourne's Countercultural Inner City Rock Scene of the '70s*, Warner Music Australia.

Laing, S. (2016), 'Liner Notes', *The Glory Days of Aussie Pub Rock*, Festival Records.

Madora, R. (2014), 'Bass Players To Know: Bill Wyman', *No Trouble*, 3 October. Available online: https://www.notreble. com/buzz/2014/10/03/bass-players-to-know-bill-wyman/ (accessed 17 June 2022).

Marx, J. (2008), 'Thirteen Tonne Theory – The Australian Review', *True Believers: Hunters and Collectors*, 5 March. Available online: https://humanfrailty.com.au/?page_id=3685 (accessed 9 June 2022).

McCredden, L. (2008), 'Sacred Violence in the Chamberlain Case', *Antipodes*, 22 (2): 117–22.

Michaud, J. (2018), 'The Miracle of Van Morrison's *Astral Weeks*', *The New Yorker*, 7 March. Available online: https://www.newyorker .com/culture/culture-desk/the-miracle-of-van-morrisons -astral-weeks (accessed 13 June 2022).

Milesago. (undated (a)), 'Billy Thorpe/The Aztecs', *Milesago.com* . Available online: http://www.milesago.com/venues/catcher .htm (accessed 13 June 2022).

Milesago. (undated (b)), 'Catcher', *Milesago.com*. Available online: http://www.milesago.com/artists/thorpe.htm (accessed 13 June 2022).

Morris, B. (2013), *Land Rights and Riots: Postcolonial Struggles in Australia in the 1980s*, New York: Berghahn Books.

Murray, J. (2011), 'Liz Reed Rock Photo Exhibition', *Tone Deaf*,
    29 July. Available online: https://tonedeaf.thebrag.com/liz
    -reed-rock-photo-exhibition/ (accessed 14 June 2022).

Nicholson, L. (1981), '"The personal is political": an analysis in
    retrospect', *Social Theory and Practice*, 7 (1): 85–98.

O. (2014). '40 Years of The Angels: A Long Line', *Rip It Up*,
    11 July. Available online: https://webarchive.nla.gov.au/awa
    /20140723192620/http://pandora.nla.gov.au/pan/134238
    /20140724-0001/www.ripitup.com.au/music/article/40-years
    -of-the-angels-a-long-line.html (accessed 13 June 2022).

O'Donnell, J., T. Cresswell, and C. Mathieson (2010), *The 100 Best
    Australian Albums*, Richmond: Hardie Grant Books.

O'Grady, A. (2016), 'Liner Notes', *The Glory Days of Aussie Pub Rock*,
    Festival Records.

O'Hanlon, S. and S. Sharpe (2009), 'Becoming Post-Industrial:
    Victoria Street, Fitzroy, *c.*1970-Now', *Urban Policy and Research*,
    27 (3): 289–300.

O'Malley, S. (2018), 'Chrism Mass Homily: Cardinal Seán O'Malley',
    *Cancao Nova*, 29 March. Available online: https://blog
    .cancaonova.com/catholicismanew/2018/03/29/chrism-mass
    -homily-cardinal-sean-omalley/ (accessed 13 June 2022).

Oldham, P. (2014), '"Suck More Piss": How the Confluence of Key
    Melbourne-based Audiences, Musicians and Iconic Scene
    Spaces Informed the Oz Rock Identity', *Perfect Beat*, 14 (2):
    120–39.

Pearce, C. N. (1981), 'Hunters and Collectors Review', *Roadrunner*,
    November.

Reynolds, S. (1987), 'End of the Track, Albums Round Up
    Column', *New Statesman*, 13 February. Available online: http://
    reynoldsretro.blogspot.com/2013/05/end-of-track-albums
    -round-up-column-new.html (accessed 25 May 2022).

Reynolds, S. (1996), 'Krautrock', *Melody Maker*, July. Available online: http://reynoldsretro.blogspot.com/2013/03/krautrock-melody-maker-july-1996-by.html (accessed 10 June 2022).

Rho-Xs. (2018), 'RhoDeo 1804 Aetix', *Rho-Xs*, 31 January. Available online: http://rho-xs.blogspot.com/2018/01/hello-todays-artists-australian-rock.html (accessed 9 June 2022).

Riley, R. (1994), 'Taking Control of Resources', in C. Fletcher (ed.), *Aboriginal Self-Determination in Australia*, 167–76, Acton, ACT: Aboriginal Studies Press.

Rock Portraits. (2014), 'Human Frailty in Rock Portraits: Hunters and Collectors'. On the web at https://rockportraits.wordpress.com/2014/09/29/hunters-and-collectors/

Ruhlmann, W. (undated), '*Astral Weeks* Review by William Ruhlmann', *AllMusic*. Available online: https://www.allmusic.com/album/astral-weeks-mw0000190975 (accessed 13 June 2022).

Seymour, M. (1985), 'Interview with Russell Brown', *Rip It Up*, 1 March. Available online: https://paperspast.natlib.govt.nz/periodicals/RIU19850301.2.28?end_date=31-12-1985&items_per_page=10&page=15&start_date=01-01-1977&title=RIU (accessed 17 June 2022).

Seymour, M. (2003), 'Liner Notes: *Natural Selection/Greatest Hits*', *True Believers: Hunters and Collectors*. Available online: https://humanfrailty.com.au/?page_id=536 (accessed 10 June 2022).

Seymour, M. (2009), *Thirteen Tonne Theory: Life Inside Hunters & Collectors*, Camberwell, VIC: Penguin Books.

Seymour, M. (undated), 'About: Silence', *MarkSeymour.com.au*. Available online: https://markseymour.com.au/about (accessed 13 June 2022).

Simic, Z. (2020), 'Rock Star in Space', in D. Nicholls and S. Perillo (eds), *Urban Australia and Post-Punk: Exploring Dogs in Space*, 105–22, London: Palgrave Macmillan.

Sly, L. (1986), '*Sonics Interview – Human Frailty*', *True Believers: Hunters and Collectors*, July/August. Available online: https://humanfrailty.com.au/?page_id=3523 (accessed 25 May 2022).

Sokol, T. (2021), 'How Charlie Watts defined the Rolling Stones' sound', *Den of Geek*, 24 August. Available online: https://www.denofgeek.com/culture/how-charlie-watts-defined-the-rolling-stones-sound-music/ (accessed 16 June 2022).

Stratton, J (forthcoming), 'Vanda and Young and the English Influence on Oz Rock in Sydney', in A. Bennett and J. Stratton (eds), *Pub Rock in the UK and Australia*, Routledge.

Tait, J. (2010). *Vanda & Young: Inside Australia's Hit Factory*, Randwick, NSW: NewSouth Publishing.

Taylor, P. (undated), 'Earwax – Live Music in Melbourne', *Phillip Taylor*. Available online: https://philliprtaylor.com/earwax-introduction/ (accessed 25 May 2022).

True Believers (undated (a)), 'Hunters and Collectors – Throw Your Arms Around Me', *True Believers: Hunters and Collectors*. Available online: https://humanfrailty.com.au/?page_id=1618 (accessed 13 June 2022).

True Believers (undated (b)), 'Mark Seymour – The Way Young Lovers Do', *True Believers: Hunters and Collectors*. Available online: https://humanfrailty.com.au/?page_id=1664 (accessed 13 June 2022).

Turner, G. (1992), 'Australian Popular Music and Its Contexts', in P. Hayward (ed.), *From Pop to Punk to Postmodernism: Popular Music and Australian Culture from the 1960s to the 1990s*, 11–24, North Sydney: Allen & Unwin.

Vincent, R. (1996), *Funk: The Music, the People and the Rhythm of the One*, New York: St Martin's Press.

Walker, C. (2005 [1981]), *Inner City Sound: Punk and Post-Punk in Australia, 1976–1985*, Portland, OR: Verse Chorus Press.

Wikipedia (2022), 'Little Band Scene', *Wikipedia*, 7 February.
Available online: https://en.wikipedia.org/wiki/Little_Band
_scene (accessed 25 May 2022).

Williams, J. (2018), 'Earthing, Energy and the Elements',
*Fire Up Water Down*, 17 June. Available online: https://
fireupwaterdown.com/2018/06/17/feet-energy-and-the
-elements/ (accessed 13 June 2022).

Wilson, E. (2021), 'A Lyrical Voice in Hollywood: French horn solos
in film 1954-2012', PhD thesis, University of California, Los
Angeles, 7 February. Available online: https://escholarship.org/
content/qt6j60c1zq/qt6j60c1zq_noSplash_453ade2db11a877
ba4e63bdf5ece1217.pdf (accessed 16 June 2022).

Winterson, J. (1987), *The Passion*, New York: Atlantic Monthly Press.

Yourgoingtohear meroar (2019), 'Throw Your Arms Around Me
- Hunters and Collectors', *YouTube*. Available online: https://
www.youtube.com/watch?v=e69wQsfrbSU (accessed 13 June
2022).

# Index